Founder Mode

Founder Mode

Leading with Resilience, Vision, and Purpose

Jon Smith

BAL
KON
media

FOUNDER MODE:
LEADING WITH RESILIENCE, VISION AND PURPOSE

Published by Balkon Media

Paperback edition ISBN: 978-1-916970-05-2
Hardcover edition ISBN: 978-1-916970-06-9
Also available in e-book format

A CIP catalogue record for this title is available from the British Library.

www.balkon.media

Also by Jon Smith

Start an Online Business in easy steps

Digital Marketing for Businesses in easy steps

Get into bed with Google

Google Adwords That Work

Dominate your market with Twitter

Smarter business start-ups

Web Sites That Work

The Power and Peril of Founder Mode

Founder Mode: Leading with Resilience, Vision, and Purpose celebrates a unique and powerful approach to leadership, one defined by passion, resilience, and an unrelenting focus on innovation. When in founder mode, leaders are deeply embedded in every facet of their business—guiding the vision, fostering direct relationships with customers, and maintaining hands-on control over decisions, especially during the critical early stages. This intense personal investment often drives some of the most successful companies, especially in fast-moving industries. The successes of entrepreneurs like Steve Jobs, who famously guided every major product decision at Apple, or Sara Blakely, who built Spanx by staying directly involved in all aspects of the business, illustrate the immense potential of founder-led companies to revolutionise industries and change the world.

In founder mode, there is a visceral commitment to the company's vision that fuels innovation and grit. Founders bring not just operational oversight, but the kind of creative energy and resourcefulness that transform businesses from ideas into global enterprises. This mode of leadership is what has driven the rapid growth of companies like Shopify, under Tobias Lütke's relentless focus on empowering entrepreneurs, and Glossier, led by Emily Weiss, whose direct connection to her customers fuelled the brand's disruptive success in beauty. The inherent ability to break from traditional rules, embrace risk, and push boundaries is what makes founder mode indispensable in the startup phase, where speed, agility, and direct oversight can make or break a company.

However, the very qualities that make founder mode powerful can, if left unchecked, lead to significant challenges. Founders who remain too deeply entrenched in every decision can stifle their team's growth, inhibit scalability, and risk missing crucial insights that come from external perspectives. Companies that fail to evolve from this mode often find themselves struggling to transition from scrappy startups into sustainable, scalable organisations. When founder mode becomes too rigid, it can foster an echo chamber, where the founder's ideas go unchallenged, leading to potential blind spots, as seen in examples like Theranos, where Elizabeth Holmes' lack of openness to dissenting opinions resulted in catastrophic failures. As businesses grow, leaders must learn to balance the hands-on approach that defines founder mode with strategic delegation and openness to diverse perspectives. The most successful founders evolve their leadership style, bringing in strong executive teams, embracing constructive feedback, and scaling their vision without losing the spark that drove their early success. This book explores the core principles of founder mode—why it matters, how it fuels growth, and the potential risks it carries if not properly balanced.

Ultimately, *Founder Mode* is a celebration of this uniquely entrepreneurial approach to leadership, while acknowledging the delicate balance required to prevent it from becoming a limitation. In a world where innovation is accelerating, founders who master this balance will be the ones who not only build successful businesses but also redefine industries and shape the future.

SECTION ONE

Foundations of Founder Mode

Chapter 1
Introduction to the Founder Mindset

The concept of the *Founder Mindset* is essential to understanding how successful entrepreneurs navigate the complexities of building and growing a business. Unlike traditional managers, founders operate with a unique blend of vision, intuition, and resilience. This mindset is more than just a style of leadership; it's a way of thinking, decision-making, and problem-solving that directly impacts the trajectory of the business.

At its core, the founder mindset is characterised by three key qualities: visionary thinking, risk tolerance, and relentless execution. These elements define how founders approach challenges, seize opportunities, and navigate the ever-changing business landscape. The intensity and personal investment that founders bring to their work set them apart from managers, who often operate within established frameworks and processes.

Visionary Thinking

Founders tend to think in terms of possibilities rather than limitations. While managers focus on optimising existing systems and processes, founders imagine *what could be.* This visionary thinking often stems from a deep belief in the potential for transformation— whether in an industry, a product, or the world itself. For many founders, the idea of creating something entirely new is what drives them, even when the odds are against them.

For founders, this kind of visionary thinking isn't just an ideal; it becomes a compass that guides the company's strategic decisions. By setting ambitious goals and pursuing innovative ideas, founders inspire their teams and attract early adopters, partners, and investors who believe in the vision. This ability to see beyond what's immediately possible is a hallmark of the founder mindset.

Risk Tolerance

Founders are known for their high tolerance for risk, which stems from their deep personal investment in the success of their ventures. Unlike managers, who often aim to minimise risk through established protocols, founders embrace uncertainty as part of the journey. For them, the possibility of failure is not something to be feared but rather a necessary step toward innovation.

The founder's comfort with risk is deeply tied to their sense of ownership and responsibility. Founders typically have much more at stake than a salaried manager. They have invested not only their financial resources but also their time, reputation, and emotional energy into the success of their company. This leads them to be more willing to take bold risks, because the upside of success aligns directly with their personal goals and vision.

For example, Sara Blakely, the founder of Spanx, risked her savings to start her business when she saw an opportunity to create a product that didn't exist in the market. Despite facing rejections from male executives who didn't understand the concept of shapewear for women, Blakely continued to push forward. Her willingness to take personal and financial risks paid off, as Spanx revolutionised the industry and made her one of the most successful self-made female entrepreneurs.

This mindset is also reflected in how founders approach market conditions. Many successful founders have a contrarian streak; they're willing to take risks on ideas or business models that others dismiss. In doing so, they often redefine industries or create entirely new categories. The ability to take calculated risks, while maintaining the conviction to see them through, is a defining trait of the founder mindset.

Relentless Execution

Perhaps the most visible aspect of the founder mindset is the founder's relentless focus on execution. Vision and risk tolerance are crucial, but without the ability to bring ideas to life, they are merely abstract qualities. Founders often distinguish themselves through their ability to get things done—no matter the obstacles.

This relentless execution is rooted in an intense personal drive and sense of accountability. Founders typically operate with a "do whatever it takes" mentality, particularly in the early stages of a company when resources are limited, and the founder must wear many hats. Whether it's coding the first version of a product, pitching to investors, founder-led sales, or handling customer support, founders are deeply involved in the day-to-day operations of their business.

Relentless execution also manifests in how founders respond to failure. The founder mindset does not treat failure as the end of the road, but rather as an opportunity to iterate and improve. Founders tend to be highly resilient, quickly learning from mistakes and pivoting when necessary to keep their business on course. This ability to adapt and execute despite setbacks is one of the reasons why so many successful founders continue to thrive even after facing early challenges.

One example of relentless execution is Jeff Bezos during the early days of Amazon. Bezos was famously involved in almost every aspect of the business, from packing boxes to answering customer service calls. His dedication to execution laid the groundwork for Amazon's customer-centric approach and operational excellence, which have been critical to its long-term success.

This focus on execution is also what sets founders apart from professional managers. Founders are builders. They create and grow companies through constant action, iteration, and hands-on involvement. The founder mindset is all about making things happen, regardless of the challenges or uncertainties involved.

Founder Mode in the High-Pressure Startup Environment

The startup environment is uniquely suited to the founder mindset because it demands a level of flexibility, adaptability, and creativity that is not typically required in more established companies. Startups operate in a space defined by uncertainty. Whether it's uncertain product-market fit, unproven business models, or volatile market conditions, the founder's ability to thrive in ambiguity sets them apart.

In the early days of a startup, every decision can be critical. There is often no existing playbook to follow, and the margin for error is narrow. In this environment, founders must navigate a combination of limited resources, constant pressure to grow, and the need to pivot quickly based on market feedback. The founder mindset excels here because it embraces this chaos as part of the process.

Startups require leaders who can handle this pressure with a level of personal ownership that goes beyond mere responsibility. Founders are typically involved in every aspect of the business, from product development and customer relations to financing and team building. The need to juggle these roles, often without established processes or systems, and without a full complement of staff, puts extraordinary demands on the founder's time and energy.

This environment is what drives many founders to adopt a "whatever it takes" approach to problem-solving. The founder mindset recognises that in a startup, progress is often made through sheer perseverance, trial and error, and an unyielding focus on the end goal. Unlike in manager mode, where decisions can be slower and more methodical, founders must act quickly to seize opportunities and address challenges as they arise. The high-stakes nature of the startup environment rewards leaders who can make quick decisions, often with limited data, and who can execute.

One prominent example of a founder thriving in this chaotic environment is Reed Hastings, the co-founder of Netflix. In its early days, Netflix was far from the streaming giant we know today. It started as a DVD rental service, and Hastings had to navigate numerous challenges to keep the business afloat. From negotiating with studios to experimenting with subscription models, Hastings demonstrated the adaptability and quick decision-making that define the founder mindset. His ability to pivot Netflix's business model from physical DVDs to online streaming at just the right time highlights how critical it is for founders to stay flexible and open to new possibilities.

The Role of Founders in Shaping Culture and Vision

One of the most critical aspects of the founder mindset in the startup environment is the founder's role in shaping the company's culture and vision. Unlike professional managers who tend to inherit a company's culture and values, founders are tasked with creating these elements from scratch. This is not only a practical necessity but also an opportunity for founders to embed their personal values and beliefs into the company.

Culture is often referred to as the "invisible hand" that guides a company, and the culture a founder creates can influence everything from how teams work together to how they respond to adversity. Founders typically build cultures around their own personality traits, preferences, and working style. In many ways, the startup's culture becomes an extension of the founder's mindset, with qualities like passion, resilience, creativity, and customer obsession often mirrored in the company's ethos.

The founder's vision, meanwhile, acts as a North Star, guiding not just the product or service but also the overall mission of the company. In a startup, this vision is often the key driver of early success. Founders with a clear and compelling vision can inspire their teams to work harder, even in the face of adversity, and can attract investors, partners, and customers who buy into that vision. Unlike professional managers, whose role is often to execute on a pre-defined strategy, founders must create that strategy and continuously communicate it to their teams.

The founder's role in shaping culture and vision can't be over-stated. It's often the founder's personal commitment to the vision that keeps the startup moving forward, even when resources are scarce, and success is uncertain. This deep connection to the company's mission is what drives founders to work long hours, make personal sacrifices, and persevere in the face of adversity.

Adaptability: The Key to Surviving Scale

As startups grow and evolve, the challenges founders face also change. While the early days are marked by chaos and rapid iteration, growth introduces a new set of complexities. Founders must adapt to these new challenges without losing the essence of what made their company successful in the first place.

One of the most important qualities of a founder mindset is adaptability. Founders who are too rigid in their thinking or who refuse to delegate responsibilities may struggle as their company scales. In the beginning, it may be possible for the founder to handle multiple roles and make all key decisions, but as the team grows, this approach becomes unsustainable. The founder must learn to build systems and processes that allow for delegation without completely relinquishing control of the company's direction.

Founders often face a critical moment when they must decide how involved they want to remain in the day-to-day operations of the company. Some choose to bring in professional managers to handle the operational aspects of the business while they focus on high-level strategy and vision. Others continue to be deeply involved in the details of their company, maintaining close relationships with employees and customers alike.

The key challenge for founders is knowing when and how to shift gears as the company grows. While staying hands-on is important in the early stages, founders need to develop a leadership style that allows for more structured growth. This doesn't mean abandoning the founder mindset but rather evolving it to meet the needs of a larger organisation. Founders who can adapt their leadership style without losing their vision and passion are often the ones who successfully navigate the transition from startup to scale-up.

Adaptability is not just about scaling leadership but also about responding to changing market conditions. Startups often operate in fast-moving industries, where customer preferences, technology, and competitors can shift quickly. Those who are too rigid in their approach may find themselves left behind, while adaptable founders can turn challenges into opportunities.

Resilience: The Backbone of the Founder Mindset

The journey of building a business is riddled with obstacles, setbacks, and moments of doubt, and it is the founder's ability to push through these challenges that often determines the company's fate. Resilience isn't just about bouncing back from failure; it's about maintaining focus and motivation even when the path forward seems unclear.

In the startup world, failure is often part of the journey. Resilient founders understand that setbacks are temporary and that success requires persistence. This mindset is especially important in industries like technology, where innovation often involves trial and error. Thomas Edison's famous quote, "I have not failed. I've just found 10,000 ways that won't work," encapsulates this resilient mindset. Founders must be willing to fail repeatedly before they find the solution that works.

Creativity: Finding Solutions Where Others See Problems

Creativity is another hallmark trait of successful founders. In many cases, founders create companies not just to fill gaps in the market, but to solve problems in new and innovative ways. Their ability to think outside the box is what allows them to disrupt industries and build products or services that capture the imagination of consumers.

Creative problem-solving is essential in the startup environment, where resources are often limited, and founders must find unconventional solutions to overcome obstacles. This creativity often manifests in the ability to turn challenges into opportunities. Where others might see insurmountable problems, founders see the chance to innovate and differentiate their company.

Creativity in the founder mindset isn't limited to product development. It also extends to how founders build teams, structure organisations, and approach growth. Founders often need to be resourceful and think creatively about how to maximise the impact of limited resources. This can mean finding new ways to motivate employees, securing unconventional partnerships, or identifying non-traditional funding sources. Creative founders are constantly looking for ways to solve problems that others might overlook, and this ingenuity is often what enables their companies to grow and succeed.

Emotional Intelligence: Building Relationships and Leading Teams

While technical skills and business acumen are important, emotional intelligence (EQ) is often the trait that sets great founders apart from the rest. Founders with high EQ are adept at managing their own emotions, as well as understanding and influencing the emotions of others. This is crucial in leadership roles, where founders must motivate teams, navigate conflicts, and build strong relationships with stakeholders.

Emotional intelligence plays a significant role in how founders handle the inevitable stresses of running a company. Founders who are self-aware and able to regulate their emotions are better equipped to deal with the pressures of leadership. They can remain calm and focused in high-pressure situations, which not only helps them make better decisions but also sets a positive example for their team. By managing their own emotional state, founders can lead with confidence and composure, even in times of uncertainty.

In addition to self-management, emotional intelligence is vital in managing relationships. Successful founders are often those who can build strong, trusting relationships with their employees, customers, investors, and partners. This requires a deep understanding of others' motivations, concerns, and aspirations. Founders with high emotional intelligence can inspire loyalty and commitment from their teams because they create an environment where people feel valued and understood.

Persistence: The Drive to Keep Going No Matter What

Starting and growing a company is rarely a linear journey. There are countless setbacks along the way—whether it's a failed product launch, difficulty raising capital, or losing key clients. Founders who succeed are those who keep going despite these setbacks.

Persistence is often linked to passion. Founders who are deeply passionate about their business are more likely to persevere through the tough times because they are personally invested in the success of their venture. This passion fuels their determination and willingness to keep pushing forward, even when the odds are stacked against them.

Persistent founders are often those who can break down large, seemingly insurmountable goals into smaller, more manageable tasks. By focusing on incremental progress and celebrating small wins along the way, they maintain their momentum and motivation. Persistence also means being able to pivot and adapt when things aren't working, rather than giving up entirely.

Managing Stress and Adversity

The founder journey is inherently stressful. The combination of high stakes, uncertainty, and personal responsibility creates a pressure-cooker environment that can take a toll on a founder's mental and physical health. Successful founders are those who learn to manage this stress in a healthy way, ensuring that they can sustain their energy and focus over the long term.

Managing stress doesn't mean avoiding it altogether; it means developing coping strategies that allow founders to maintain clarity and resilience in the face of adversity. This can include everything from time management techniques to mindfulness practices, as well as seeking support from mentors, peers, or mental health professionals.

Arianna Huffington, the founder of The Huffington Post, is a notable advocate for stress management among founders. After collapsing from exhaustion in the early years of her company, Huffington realised that burnout was unsustainable and began advocating for better work-life balance in the entrepreneurial community. Her experience underscores the importance of self-care and stress management for founders who are in it for the long haul.

Chapter 2
Why Founder Mode Matters: The Evolution of Leadership

Leadership in business has undergone significant transformations over the last century. From the rigid hierarchies of early industrial organisations to the flexible, innovation-driven models seen today, the concept of leadership has shifted in response to changing market dynamics, technological advancements, and societal expectations. Central to this evolution is the emergence of what we now call *Founder Mode*—a hands-on, visionary approach to leadership that contrasts sharply with the more traditional *Manager Mode*.

To understand why founder mode matters, it's essential to first explore the historical context of leadership and how it has evolved. Early leadership models were shaped by the needs of large, bureaucratic organisations that prioritised efficiency, standardisation, and control. The rise of the industrial revolution in the late 19th and early 20th centuries gave birth to large corporations where leadership was defined by hierarchy, authority, and a clear division of labour.

Frederick Taylor's theory of *Scientific Management* was one of the most influential models of leadership in the early 20th century. Taylor advocated for breaking down tasks into simple, repetitive motions that could be measured and optimised. Workers were seen as cogs in a larger machine, and the role of leadership was to maximise productivity by strictly controlling the work process. This approach worked well in industries like manufacturing, where efficiency and consistency were critical, but it left little room for innovation or creativity.

As industries grew more complex and globalised in the mid-20th century, leadership theories began to evolve. Peter Drucker, often considered the father of modern management, introduced ideas that expanded the role of leaders beyond mere task management. Drucker emphasised the importance of the *knowledge worker* and the need for leaders to motivate, inspire, and develop their teams. This shift marked the beginning of a more human-centred approach to leadership, where emotional intelligence, collaboration, and adaptability began to play a larger role.

However, even as these ideas gained traction, leadership remained largely hierarchical and management-driven. The role of the CEO or executive team was to set high-level goals and strategies, leaving day-to-day decision-making to middle managers and other department heads. This structure worked well in stable industries where predictability and process optimisation were paramount.

But as the pace of technological change accelerated in the late 20th and early 21st centuries, this approach to leadership began to show its limitations. The rise of the internet, globalisation, and rapid innovation meant that businesses had to be more nimble, adaptable, and creative. It was no longer enough to optimise for efficiency; companies needed to innovate and disrupt to stay ahead. This is where the *founder mindset* began to take centre stage.

The Shift from Managerial Leadership to Founder Leadership

The late 20th century saw the rise of iconic founders like Steve Jobs, Bill Gates, and Richard Branson, who transformed entire industries through their visionary leadership. These founders were not content to simply manage; they were deeply involved in shaping every aspect of their companies, from product design to customer experience. Their leadership style broke away from the traditional manager mode, which focused on delegation, control, and maintaining the status quo.

Founders, in contrast, thrive on *disruption*. They seek to challenge existing norms, create new markets, and solve problems in ways that no one else has imagined. This requires a leadership style that is agile, risk-tolerant, and deeply connected to the core mission of the company. While traditional managers are often focused on maintaining operational efficiency, founders are focused on building something new.

The transition from managerial leadership to founder leadership became especially apparent during the tech boom of the 1990s and early 2000s. Companies like Apple, Microsoft, and Amazon grew rapidly, not because they followed traditional management practices, but because their founders were willing to take risks and innovate. Jeff Bezos, for example, was not content to build a better bookstore; he envisioned Amazon as a platform that would eventually dominate online retail, cloud computing, and media.

Bezos's ability to think beyond the immediate market opportunity and focus on long-term disruption exemplifies the founder mindset. Unlike traditional CEOs, who might prioritise short-term profits or incremental growth, founders like Bezos are willing to make bold, sometimes counterintuitive bets that can reshape entire industries. This visionary thinking is what sets founder mode apart from manager mode and is a key reason why founder-led companies often outperform those led by professional managers.

The Modern Founder: Disruptors and Innovators

As business landscapes continue to evolve in the 21st century, the role of the founder has shifted dramatically once again, cementing them as key disruptors and innovators. Modern founders challenge not just the markets they enter but also the very nature of how businesses are run. Their impact goes beyond mere profitability; they influence societal norms, disrupt traditional industries, and often spark conversations about the future of work, technology, and human behaviour.

Founders as Disruptors

Modern founders are not merely concerned with improving an existing product or service—they are focused on breaking away from conventional systems entirely. These leaders often find success not by iterating on current solutions but by completely rethinking how industries operate. One of the most prominent examples of this is Elon Musk, the founder of The Boring Company and SpaceX. Musk's leadership is a textbook case of founder mode in action—he refuses to accept the limitations of current technology, whether it's in electric vehicles, space travel, or energy storage.

Monzo wasn't the first digital bank, but Tom Blomfield's vision extended far beyond traditional banking services. Blomfield set out to reinvent banking by focusing on transparency, customer experience, and financial empowerment through technology. From real-time spending notifications to no-fee international transactions, Monzo disrupted the financial services industry by offering a product that was deeply user-centric. Monzo didn't just build a bank; it created a community-driven platform that reshaped how people engage with their financesE.

Elon Musk's work at SpaceX is another powerful example of disruption. His goal wasn't simply to make space travel more affordable but to open up the possibility of colonising Mars, a vision that sounds more like science fiction than reality. Yet, his relentless pursuit of this goal has pushed SpaceX to innovate in ways, and at a speed, that traditional aerospace companies could not. Reusable rockets, something that was once thought impossible, are now a key part of SpaceX's business model, enabling significant cost reductions in space missions.

Musk's example illustrates the core of founder mode: a willingness to take extreme risks and to challenge the status quo. This mindset contrasts sharply with traditional managerial leadership, where risk is often minimised in favour of incremental improvement. For modern founders, the focus is not on maintaining the status quo but on creating something entirely new—something that disrupts the current market and forces industries to adapt or become obsolete.

The Airbnb Story: Innovation in Business Models

Another prime example of modern founders as disruptors is Brian Chesky of Airbnb. Like many founders, Chesky saw an opportunity where others saw risk or impossibility. Airbnb started as a simple idea: what if people could rent out their homes to travellers? In the early days, Chesky faced significant scepticism—not only from investors but also from consumers and regulators. The hospitality industry was dominated by large hotel chains, and the idea that people would willingly stay in a stranger's home seemed far-fetched to many.

But Chesky's vision went beyond just short-term rentals; he wanted to build a community of travellers and hosts who could connect on a personal level. His leadership style reflected the founder mode ethos—he was deeply involved in every aspect of the company, from designing the user interface to personally recruiting hosts in the early days. Chesky's hands-on approach, combined with his ability to see the potential for Airbnb to disrupt the hotel industry, was critical to the company's success.

Airbnb is now a global platform, and its impact on the travel industry has been profound. Hotel chains have been forced to adapt their business models to compete with the flexibility and affordability that Airbnb offers. Additionally, cities around the world have had to grapple with new regulations to address the rise of short-term rentals, something that was barely on the radar before Airbnb's disruption.

Chesky's leadership demonstrates another key aspect of founder mode: the ability to adapt and pivot as necessary. In 2020, when the global lockdown devastated the travel industry, Airbnb faced a crisis that could have crippled the company. But instead of retreating, Chesky doubled down on his vision for the future of travel. Airbnb pivoted to focus on long-term stays and rural travel, capitalising on the new demand for remote work and longer stays outside of urban areas. This flexibility and willingness to evolve in the face of external challenges is a hallmark of successful founders.

Balancing Innovation with Operational Efficiency

While founders are known for their visionary thinking and disruptive ideas, scaling these innovations into sustainable business models requires balancing that innovation with operational efficiency. This is where many founders struggle, as the shift from startup to scale-up introduces new challenges. Companies that begin as scrappy, agile startups must eventually introduce more formal structures, processes, and teams to maintain operational efficiency.

However, what sets great founders apart is their ability to maintain their focus on innovation while scaling their operations. Jeff Bezos is a perfect example of a leader who has balanced both. From its humble beginnings as an online bookstore, Bezos grew Amazon into one of the most valuable companies in the world, encompassing everything from cloud computing to entertainment.

Bezos's leadership at Amazon has been marked by a dual focus: on the one hand, relentless innovation, as seen in projects like Amazon Web Services (AWS), Prime, and the company's foray into AI with Alexa; on the other hand, a focus on operational excellence, such as the development of Amazon's world-class supply chain and logistics infrastructure. This combination of long-term visionary thinking, and short-term execution, has made Amazon a dominant player across multiple industries.

For Bezos, maintaining this balance involved creating a culture that embraced experimentation while optimising operations. Amazon famously operates with a "Day 1" philosophy, which encourages employees to think like a startup even as the company has grown to over a million employees. Bezos's ability to infuse the company with an entrepreneurial spirit while maintaining operational efficiency is a model for modern founder leadership.

Redefining Leadership in the 21st Century

Modern founders are not just business leaders—they are redefining what leadership looks like in the 21st century. In traditional corporate environments, leadership has often been synonymous with hierarchy, structure, and delegation. But in the world of startups and disruptive businesses, leadership has become more fluid, collaborative, and visionary.

Founders like Musk, Chesky, and Bezos demonstrate that leadership in the modern era is about more than just managing people or resources—it's about inspiring teams, challenging conventional wisdom, and driving innovation. This new model of leadership prioritises adaptability, customer obsession, and long-term thinking over short-term profits and stability.

Moreover, these founders have reshaped the expectations of what it means to be a leader. In the past, business leaders were often expected to maintain a certain distance from the day-to-day operations of their companies, delegating responsibilities to middle managers and encouraged to enjoy the perks of being the boss, by becoming 'hands off'. In contrast, modern founders are "hands on", often deeply involved in the nitty-gritty of their businesses, from user experience (UX) to customer success. This level of engagement sets a new standard for leadership, where founders are not just figureheads but active participants in every aspect of their companies.

Jon Smith

Founder Mode and Its Influence on Business Education and Leadership Programmes

As the influence of founder-led companies continues to grow, it is becoming increasingly clear that the traditional business education model is evolving in response. Business schools, long focused on teaching long-established management theory, operational efficiency, and strategic planning, are starting to integrate more entrepreneurial thinking into their curricula. The rise of *founder mode* as a leadership style has begun to reshape how leadership is taught, with an increasing emphasis on innovation, risk-taking, and agility.

Consider the rise of entrepreneurship programmes in major US business schools such as Stanford's Graduate School of Business and the Massachusetts Institute of Technology's Sloan School of Management. Both institutions have expanded their focus on founder-driven leadership by offering courses that teach students how to think and act like founders. These programmes place a strong emphasis on design thinking, innovation, and disruptive business models. Of course, not all of these graduates will go on to become founders, but they will take their learnings with them to their individual contributor roles, middle management positions, or seats on the executive team. By encouraging students to adopt the mindset of a founder, these schools are preparing future leaders to navigate a rapidly changing business landscape —and begin, or continue, their careers with *founder mode* activated.

Additionally, these programmes are increasingly focused on *experiential learning*, a teaching methodology that mimics the experience of starting a business. Students are given opportunities to develop real-world projects, launch startups, and work through the challenges founders face in their early stages. The ability to experience failure in a controlled environment is particularly important in fostering a founder mindset, as many successful founders attribute their eventual success to learning from early failures.

This shift in education is not just limited to business schools.

Corporate leadership programmes are also adapting to incorporate principles of founder mode. Companies like Google and Slack have launched internal leadership initiatives that encourage employees to think like entrepreneurs, even within large, established organisations. Google's famous 20% time policy, which allows employees to spend one day a week working on passion projects unrelated to their core job, is a direct result of this shift. This policy has led to some of Google's most successful products, including Gmail and Google News.

The long-term impact of these educational shifts is profound. As more leaders are trained to think and act like founders, businesses across industries will likely see a rise in innovation, agility, and resilience. The rigid, process-driven leadership models of the past are being replaced by more dynamic and responsive approaches, shaped by the principles of founder mode.

Founder Mode and Shareholder Expectations

The rise of founder mode has also begun to change the expectations of shareholders and investors. Traditionally, investors prioritised short-term returns, focusing on profitability, cost control, and quarterly earnings. However, as founder-led companies have demonstrated, long-term vision and innovation often deliver greater value over time, even if it means sacrificing short-term profits.

Take the example of Indra Nooyi, the former CEO and Chairperson of PepsiCo, who adopted a founder-like mindset even in a massive, established corporation. Nooyi led a shift towards what she called "Performance with Purpose," integrating long-term sustainability and health-focused initiatives into PepsiCo's core strategy. She moved the company towards healthier snacks and beverages, investing in innovation that would align with shifting consumer preferences and global health trends. Initially, Nooyi's strategy was met with scepticism from shareholders, who were concerned about the impact on short-term profits and consumer confusion. However, her visionary approach ultimately paid off, as PepsiCo experienced steady growth and strengthened its reputation as a forward-thinking company.

This shift towards long-term thinking is becoming more common among investors, particularly in sectors where innovation is critical to survival. Venture capital firms, for example, often prioritise investing in founders with bold, disruptive ideas over more established companies that may offer stable returns but little growth potential. Andreessen Horowitz, one of Silicon Valley's leading venture capital firms, famously looks for founders who "have a vision that changes the world," even if that vision might take years to realise.

Founders who can effectively communicate their long-term vision and build trust with shareholders are more likely to secure the resources needed to execute on their strategies. Whitney Wolfe Herd, the founder of Bumble, exemplifies this ability to balance innovation with investor expectations. Herd's vision for a female-centric dating platform that prioritised safety and respect disrupted the online dating industry. Despite initial pushback from investors who were uncertain about the viability of what appeared to be a niche market, Herd's leadership led Bumble to become one of the most popular dating apps globally. Herd was able to articulate a clear and compelling vision, which not only attracted users but also reassured investors about the company's long-term potential.

The Challenges and Risks of Founder Mode

While founder mode offers many benefits, it is not without its risks. One of the key challenges that founder-led companies face is the transition from a plucky startup to a more structured, scalable enterprise. The very traits that make founders successful—hands-on involvement, risk tolerance, and visionary thinking—can sometimes hinder their ability to manage larger teams or scale operations efficiently.

A notable example of this challenge is WeWork, co-founded by

Adam Neumann. Neumann's leadership was defined by his visionary thinking and bold, ambitious plans to transform office spaces around the world. However, as WeWork scaled, Neumann's inability to transition to a more structured and disciplined leadership style led to significant operational and financial issues. His reluctance to delegate and his erratic decision-making, hallmarks of founder mode, became liabilities as the company expanded. Ultimately, WeWork's IPO collapsed, and Neumann was forced to step down as CEO.

This highlights the importance of evolving leadership as a company grows. Founders must be able to recognise when their leadership style needs to adapt to meet the changing needs of the business. Successful founders often bring in experienced executives or operational leaders to manage day-to-day operations while they focus on the big picture. Evan Spiegel, the founder of Snap Inc., is a good example of a founder who has successfully navigated this transition. While Spiegel remains deeply involved in the vision and strategy of Snapchat, he has surrounded himself with seasoned executives who manage the company's operations, allowing him to maintain focus on innovation.

Additionally, founder-led companies can face governance challenges, particularly when founders hold significant control over voting shares. While founder control can allow for swift decision-making and long-term focus, it can also lead to issues if the founder's interests diverge from those of shareholders. For example, Mark Zuckerberg's control over Facebook (now Meta) has allowed him to maintain a strong grip on the company's direction, but it has also raised concerns about governance and accountability, particularly as the company faces increasing scrutiny over its role in data privacy and misinformation.

Maintaining the Entrepreneurial Spirit as Companies Scale

The final challenge that founder-led companies face is maintaining the entrepreneurial spirit as they scale. Many companies that start with a disruptive, innovative culture struggle to retain that same energy and agility as they grow. The processes and systems that are necessary for scaling can sometimes stifle the creativity and risk-taking that define founder mode.

Maintaining the entrepreneurial spirit requires a conscious effort from founders. They must continually foster a culture of innovation, encourage risk-taking, and ensure that their teams feel empowered to experiment. This can be achieved through organisational structures that prioritise agility, such as small, cross-functional teams, as well as through leadership that rewards creativity and forward thinking.

Chapter 3
Founder Mode in Silicon Valley and Beyond

Founder mode, as a leadership style, operates differently depending on the industry. While Silicon Valley's high-tech environment may be its most visible example, the principles of founder mode are also applied across a variety of other sectors. Tech founders tend to operate in a fast-paced, innovation-driven ecosystem where rapid decision-making, technological disruption, and hypergrowth are common. However, outside the tech sector, founder mode manifests differently based on industry-specific demands, such as manufacturing, retail, or even non-profit organisations.

Founder Mode in Silicon Valley: Speed, Innovation, and Hypergrowth

In Silicon Valley, where technology companies lead the charge, founder mode thrives in a culture that values rapid experimentation, constant disruption, and aggressive scaling. Founders in this environment are expected to be visionary leaders, pushing the boundaries of what's possible in tech, while simultaneously managing the fast-paced growth of their companies. The stakes are high, but so are the rewards, and this pressure drives founders to adopt a mode of leadership that is far more experimental and agile than traditional corporate models.

The emphasis on speed and innovation in Silicon Valley shapes how founder mode is practiced. In the world of application development, new ideas must be tested, launched and scaled quickly before competitors have the chance to catch up. As a result, tech founders often operate in short sprints, testing Minimum Viable Products (MVPs), gathering feedback, and iterating quickly. Failure is not only accepted—it is often encouraged as part of the learning process. In this context, founders must be highly adaptable, constantly ready to pivot when new technologies emerge or market conditions shift.

Founder mode in Silicon Valley is characterised by:

- **Fast-paced decision-making**: The ability to make rapid, high-stakes decisions in response to technological developments and market opportunities.
- **Emphasis on innovation**: Founders in tech push boundaries, often disrupting their own business models to stay ahead of the curve.
- **A tolerance for failure**: Failure is seen as a learning tool, not a detriment, allowing for constant iteration and improvement.
- **Hypergrowth**: The expectation that companies will scale rapidly, capturing market share and securing capital to drive their expansion.

Founder Mode in Other Industries: Adaptation and Differentiation

While founder mode in tech industries is defined by speed and innovation, its application in other sectors can differ significantly. Outside Silicon Valley, founder mode must adapt to the specific demands of each industry, with different approaches to leadership, growth, and risk-taking. Although the core principles of founder mode—agility, vision, and innovation—remain intact, the way they are applied varies based on factors such as the pace of industry change, market structure, access to funding, Total Addressable Markets (TAMs) and customer expectations.

Founder Mode in Retail: Innovation with Customer Focus

In the retail sector, founders must strike a balance between innovation and customer-centricity. Retail founders operate in an environment where consumer behaviour shifts rapidly, but where the physical infrastructure and supply chains often make quick pivots more difficult. As a result, retail founders tend to focus on customer experience and innovation in product offerings while using technology to streamline operations and create efficiencies.

Sara Blakely, founder of Spanx, built her company on innovative product design that addressed customer pain points—specifically, the need for comfortable, flattering shapewear. Blakely's founder mode was rooted in a deep understanding of her customers, combined with an unconventional approach to marketing and product development. Spanx's growth was driven by its ability to innovate in a crowded retail space, showing how founder mode can adapt to industries where customer satisfaction and product innovation are key.

In retail, founder mode emphasises:

- **Customer experience as a driver of innovation**: Retail founders focus on understanding and meeting customer needs in creative ways.
- **Operational efficiency**: Technology is leveraged to optimise supply chains, logistics, and inventory management to support growth.
- **Long-term brand loyalty**: While tech founders may

focus on short-term pivots, retail founders often work to build strong, lasting relationships with their customers.

Founder Mode in Manufacturing

In manufacturing, founder mode operates differently due to the capital-intensive nature of the industry and the slower pace of technological disruption. Founders in this space must focus on process innovation, ensuring that they can scale production efficiently while maintaining high-quality standards. The challenge for manufacturing founders is to adopt new technologies—such as automation, robotics, and artificial intelligence—while balancing the need for investment in physical infrastructure.

James Dyson, founder of Dyson, exemplifies a founder mode leadership style through his relentless innovation in product design, coupled with a deep understanding of manufacturing processes. His commitment to improving everyday products, from vacuum cleaners to hand dryers, required long-term investment in research and development as well as scalable production capabilities. Dyson's approach shows how founder mode can drive disruptive innovation in industries that are traditionally slower to adapt to change.

In manufacturing, founder mode emphasises:

- **Process and product innovation**: Founders focus on improving the efficiency of production processes and designing innovative products that differentiate them from competitors.
- **Long-term investment**: Founders in manufacturing often need to invest in infrastructure and technology over extended periods, making growth slower but more sustainable.
- **Scalability through technology**: Automation and robotics play a critical role in enabling manufacturing founders to scale operations efficiently.

The Global Expansion of Founder Mode

While founder mode is often associated with technology businesses, and predominantly those founded in the US, its influence has expanded globally and across various sectors. As more regions develop their startup ecosystems and entrepreneurial hubs, founders around the world are adapting the principles of founder mode to their unique cultural, economic, and industrial contexts. These founders face different challenges, such as regulatory environments, access to capital, and local market conditions, but the core elements of agility, vision, and innovation remain essential to their success.

Founder Mode in Europe: Balancing Innovation and Regulation

In Europe, startups often operate in highly regulated environments, particularly in industries such as finance, healthcare, and technology. While this can create additional hurdles for founders, the region has produced some of the world's most innovative and successful companies. European founders tend to approach founder mode with a strong focus on sustainability, ethical leadership, and compliance with regulatory standards, while still maintaining an emphasis on rapid growth and innovation.

One example of founder mode in Europe is Daniel Ek, co-founder and CEO of Spotify. Ek launched Spotify in Sweden at a time when the music industry was struggling with piracy and declining sales. By introducing a legal, user-friendly streaming platform, Ek disrupted the global music industry while navigating Europe's stringent regulations around intellectual property and digital content. Ek's approach to founder mode blended innovation with a deep understanding of the legal landscape, allowing Spotify to scale rapidly while staying compliant with local and international laws, and being able to offer music producers, rights owners and musicians a new way to earn royalties.

European founders often prioritise:

- **Sustainability and ethics**: European companies frequently lead in areas such as environmental sustainability and corporate social responsibility, integrating these values into their business models.
- **Compliance with regulations**: Startups in Europe must navigate complex regulatory environments, particularly in industries like fintech, healthcare, and data privacy (e.g., GDPR). There are also far more robust labour laws than in the US, therefore founders in these sectors need to be adaptable while ensuring that their innovations comply with legal requirements.
- **Long-term growth**: European founders may take a more measured approach to growth, focusing on building sustainable businesses that can withstand market fluctuations and regulatory changes.

Nikolay Storonsky, co-founder of Revolut, a UK-based fintech company, exemplifies this approach. Storonsky applied founder mode to disrupt traditional banking by offering digital financial services and currency exchange with lower fees. Revolut's success required navigating Europe's highly regulated financial sector while staying agile and continuously adding new services, from cryptocurrencies to investment products and currency exchange. Storonsky's ability to innovate within the confines of complex cross-border regulatory compliance demonstrates how founder mode can be adapted to fit the constraints of the European market.

Founder Mode in Asia: Scale and Adaptability

In Asia, founder mode often operates within a context of massive scale and intense competition. With large populations and rapidly developing economies, Asia presents both significant opportunities and challenges for entrepreneurs. Founders in Asia must be prepared to scale their businesses quickly to capture market share while also adapting to the diverse needs of local markets, particularly in regions with vast cultural, linguistic, and economic differences.

Jack Ma, founder of Alibaba, exemplifies founder mode in the Asian market. Ma's vision was to create an e-commerce platform that would empower small businesses across China to reach consumers around the world. However, building Alibaba required Ma to overcome significant obstacles, including a lack of trust in online transactions and logistical challenges in delivering goods from across China's vast geography internationally. Ma's leadership was marked by his ability to scale Alibaba at an unprecedented pace while adapting to the unique demands of the Chinese market and the expectations of international business customers.

Founders in Asia often focus on:

- **Rapid scaling**: Asian markets, particularly in China and India, are characterised by large populations and growing middle classes, requiring startups to scale quickly to meet demand.
- **Localisation**: Founders in Asia must adapt their products and services to cater to the diverse cultural, economic, and linguistic needs of their markets, even within a single country's Go To Market strategy. This requires flexibility in both business models and customer engagement strategies.
- **Navigating government relationships**: Many Asian countries have strong government involvement in key industries, and founders must build relationships with regulators and policymakers to ensure their businesses can operate smoothly.

Nadiem Makarim, founder of Gojek in Indonesia, showcases how founder mode can thrive in emerging Asian markets. Gojek started as a ride-hailing service and quickly expanded into a super-app offering everything from food delivery to digital payments. Makarim's ability to understand the local market and rapidly scale Gojek into a multi-service platform reflects the adaptability and vision required to succeed in the Asian tech landscape. His approach to founder mode involved deep Localisation, understanding the needs of both drivers and consumers, and leveraging technology to streamline operations in a highly fragmented market.

Founder Mode in Emerging Markets: Innovating for Local Challenges

In emerging markets across Africa, Latin America, and Southeast Asia, founder mode often centres on solving local problems through innovative business models. Founders in these regions face unique challenges such as limited infrastructure, lower access to capital, and political instability. However, these constraints also present opportunities for creative solutions that can have a significant impact on local communities and economies.

Sim Shagaya, founder of Konga, one of Nigeria's largest e-commerce platforms, exemplifies how founder mode can drive innovation in emerging markets. Shagaya launched Konga to address the challenges of shopping in Nigeria, where limited retail infrastructure and logistical issues made it difficult for consumers to access goods. By building an online marketplace and developing a reliable delivery network, Shagaya created a solution tailored to Nigeria's specific challenges. His leadership highlights the importance of local market understanding and innovation in founder mode, as Konga adapted to Nigeria's unique infrastructure and consumer needs.

Eren Bali, co-founder of Udemy, faced similar challenges when launching his company in Turkey, an emerging market at the time. Bali's vision was to create an online education platform that would democratise access to learning. However, he had to overcome significant technological and cultural barriers in Turkey, including limited internet access and scepticism about online education. Bali's perseverance and ability to adapt Udemy's model to fit local market needs allowed the company to expand globally, demonstrating how founder mode can lead to successful outcomes in emerging markets.

One of the most consistent themes across industries is the need for founders to be agile. Whether operating in Silicon Valley, Europe, Asia, or in emerging markets, founders must be ready to pivot quickly, adapt to changing circumstances, and take advantage of new opportunities. Agility enables founders to navigate uncertainty, respond to market shifts, and experiment with new ideas without being bogged down by rigid structures or long-term plans that may no longer be relevant.

Chapter 4

Visionary Leadership: The Founder as the North Star

A key characteristic that distinguishes founders from traditional executives is their role as visionary leaders. Unlike CEOs or managers brought in to run established companies, founders often have a deeply personal connection to the mission and vision of the company they built. This connection drives their decision-making and shapes the company's culture, values, and long-term direction. In essence, founders serve as the "North Star" for their organisations, providing a sense of purpose and direction that guides everything from product development to organisational behaviour.

In this chapter, we will explore the visionary role that founders play in shaping their companies, with detailed case studies of how different founders have infused their personal values and vision into their organisations. By examining the direct influence of founders on their company's mission, values, and product direction, we'll highlight how visionary leadership is essential for driving long-term success, innovation, and organisational alignment.

Founders as Visionaries: Setting the Mission and Values

One of the most critical responsibilities of a founder is to establish the mission and values of their company. These elements are not just slogans or branding tools; they are the bedrock of how the company operates and how it is perceived by customers, employees, and the wider market. Founders often craft these foundational elements based on their personal experiences, beliefs, and goals, making them unique to the company they create.

Founders who effectively communicate their mission and values help their organisations maintain focus, even as they scale. These values become a guide for decision-making and a benchmark for the type of culture the company fosters. Moreover, the founder's vision ensures that everyone—from senior leadership to front-line employees—understands what the company stands for and what it aims to achieve.

Ben Silbermann, co-founder of Pinterest, provides an excellent case study of how a founder's vision can shape the entire mission of a company. Silbermann envisioned Pinterest as a platform for people to discover new ideas and find inspiration in a positive, creative environment. This mission was deeply personal for Silbermann, who wanted to create a space where people could explore their interests without the pressure of social validation that dominates other platforms. By embedding this vision into Pinterest's DNA, Silbermann ensured that the platform's product design, content policies, and community guidelines all revolved around the idea of positivity and creativity.

Similarly, Howard Schultz, founder of Starbucks, shaped the company's mission around creating a "third place" between home and work where people could gather, relax, and enjoy high-quality coffee. Schultz's vision was rooted in his own experiences with Italian coffee culture, and he believed that Starbucks could replicate that sense of community and belonging in the United States. This mission has guided Starbucks through decades of growth, influencing everything from store design to employee training and customer service.

The clarity and focus that visionary founders bring to their organisations can serve as a powerful competitive advantage. Companies led by visionary founders tend to have stronger brand loyalty, as their mission and values resonate with customers who share the same beliefs. Moreover, these companies often attract top talent, as employees are drawn to work for organisations that have a clear sense of purpose and are led by founders who are passionate about their mission.

Whitney Wolfe Herd, founder of Bumble, is a prime example of how a founder's personal values and mission can shape not only a company's product but its entire culture. After leaving Tinder, Wolfe Herd founded Bumble with the goal of creating a dating app where women were empowered to take control of their online interactions. This mission—to empower women and challenge traditional gender dynamics—became the foundation for Bumble's product design, marketing, and company culture.

Wolfe Herd's visionary leadership led to the creation of Bumble's signature feature: only women can make the first move in heterosexual matches. This feature was a direct reflection of her mission to give women more control in the online dating space and address issues of harassment and unwanted messages. Beyond the product itself, Bumble's brand and culture are built around values of inclusivity, respect, and female empowerment.

Wolfe Herd's vision also extended beyond dating. Bumble later expanded into new areas, launching Bumble BFF for finding friends and Bumble Bizz for professional networking, all while maintaining the same values of empowerment and fostering respectful interactions. This consistent vision helped Bumble differentiate itself from other dating apps and build a loyal user base that shared, or bought into, the company's values.

Yvon Chouinard, founder of Patagonia, has been an unwavering advocate for environmental sustainability, and his personal passion for protecting the planet has been the driving force behind Patagonia's mission, culture, and innovation strategy. Chouinard's vision for Patagonia was to create a company that not only made high-quality outdoor gear but also used its business as a tool for environmental activism.

Patagonia's commitment to sustainability is evident in everything from its supply chain practices to its product design. The company prioritises the use of environmentally friendly materials, ethical manufacturing processes, and fair labour practices. Patagonia's "Worn Wear" programme, which encourages customers to repair and reuse their clothing instead of buying new items, is an example of how the company's innovation strategy aligns with its mission to reduce waste and promote environmental responsibility.

Chouinard's leadership has also shaped Patagonia's culture of activism. The company has donated significant portions of its profits to environmental causes and consistently advocates for conservation and climate change awareness. Patagonia employees are encouraged to get involved in activism, with the company even offering paid time off for them to participate in environmental initiatives. This alignment between Patagonia's mission and its day-to-day operations has fostered a strong sense of purpose within the organisation.

Chouinard's visionary leadership also guided Patagonia's product innovation. By insisting on sustainable materials and processes, Patagonia pioneered innovations like recycled polyester and organic cotton in its clothing lines. These innovations not only helped reduce the company's environmental footprint but also set an industry standard, proving that sustainability and profitability can coexist.

One of Patagonia's most notable campaigns under Chouinard's leadership was the "Don't Buy This Jacket" advertisement, which encouraged consumers to think twice before purchasing new items and promoted responsible consumption. This bold move reinforced Patagonia's commitment to environmental responsibility, even at the risk of sacrificing sales, and cemented its reputation as a purpose-driven brand.

The Challenges of Maintaining Visionary Leadership as Companies Scale

As companies grow, one of the most significant challenges founders face is maintaining their original vision and leadership style. While it's relatively easy to stay closely connected to the company's mission and product direction in the early stages, scaling introduces complexity—bigger teams, more stakeholders, operational challenges, and a broader range of responsibilities. As a result, many founders struggle to remain as hands-on and visionary as they once were.

Scaling Leadership Without Losing Vision

When scaling, a common issue arises when new managers or executives are brought in to run operations. While these hires may be necessary for growth, they can inadvertently shift the company's focus from the founder's vision to more traditional business priorities like efficiency and profitability. If left unchecked, this shift can dilute the founder's original vision and mission, leading to a loss of direction.

One way to address this challenge is for founders to focus on scaling their leadership rather than trying to do everything themselves. This means empowering key leaders within the company to understand and internalise the founder's vision. By investing in leadership development and ensuring that the company's mission is deeply ingrained in its culture, founders can scale the business while keeping the vision intact.

Delegating Without Losing Control of Product Direction

One of the hardest transitions for visionary founders is learning to delegate responsibilities without feeling like they are losing control over product direction. Early on, founders often play a central role in product development, directly shaping how their products or services are designed and brought to market. Stepping back from day-to-day decision-making can feel like a loss of control, particularly when the founder's vision has been the driving force behind the product's success.

A potential pitfall here is that as more layers of management are added, the company's product development process may become more bureaucratic or detached from the founder's original vision. This can lead to a situation where products lose the unique qualities that set them apart from competitors or where innovation stalls due to a focus on incremental improvements rather than bold new ideas.

To overcome this challenge, founders must find a balance between delegation and involvement. They should still provide strategic oversight for product direction while trusting their teams to handle the execution. One approach is to establish clear principles and guidelines that align with the company's mission, ensuring that every product decision supports the founder's vision. Founders can also stay involved in critical moments—such as major product launches or strategic pivots—without needing to micromanage daily operations.

Chapter 5
The Role of Instinct in Founder Mode

One of the most intriguing aspects of founder mode is the reliance on instinct in decision-making. While many leaders in the corporate world lean heavily on data and analysis to drive decisions, successful founders often use their intuition to make bold, unconventional choices. In founder-led companies, instinct plays a crucial role in guiding strategy, innovation, and business development, especially when data is limited or market trends are unclear. This ability to trust one's gut, even in the face of conflicting data or industry norms, can be a powerful asset, helping founders seize opportunities and navigate uncertainty.

In this chapter, we will explore how instinct influences decision-making in founder mode and why it can be highly effective. We'll look at case studies of founders who used their intuition to make counterintuitive decisions that led to significant success, demonstrating how instinct, when combined with experience and vision, can create unique competitive advantages.

Instinct vs. Data: The Founder's Dilemma

In modern business environments, data-driven decision-making is often regarded as the gold standard. From customer analytics to financial modelling, data provides a quantitative basis for evaluating risk and predicting outcomes. However, founders frequently operate in spaces where data is either scarce or unreliable, especially in emerging industries or during times of rapid innovation. In these instances, founders often rely on their instincts, drawing on personal experience, intuition, and a deep understanding of their industry to make decisions that defy conventional logic.

Instinct-driven decision-making doesn't disregard data altogether; rather, it acknowledges that data can be incomplete or misleading, especially in the early stages of a business or in new markets. Founders who trust their instincts recognise that human intuition can sometimes perceive opportunities or risks that data cannot capture. This is particularly true in scenarios involving consumer behaviour, market shifts, or new technology, where it's difficult to model future trends accurately.

One key example of a founder who leaned heavily on instinct is Richard Branson at Virgin Group. Branson's intuition has guided his business ventures across a wide range of industries, from music to airlines to space travel. Throughout his career, Branson has made decisions that often went against data or traditional business advice, yet these instinctual moves frequently paid off. For example, when Branson decided to launch Virgin Atlantic, many industry experts advised him that competing with established airlines like British Airways was too risky and that the data suggested there wasn't enough market demand. However, Branson's instinct told him that travellers wanted a better flying experience, and he launched the airline based on his belief that Virgin could offer superior service and innovation. Virgin Atlantic's success proved that Branson's gut feeling was more accurate than the industry data.

Why Instinct Matters in Founder Mode

The ability to trust one's instincts is critical in founder mode because startups often operate in environments of high uncertainty, where rapid decision-making is essential. Founders are frequently faced with ambiguous situations where there is no clear right or wrong answer, and they must rely on their intuition to make decisions quickly. This instinctive approach can be particularly effective in industries undergoing disruption or where new markets are being created, as founders are often the first to recognise emerging opportunities or shifts in consumer behaviour.

Instinct also plays a vital role in innovation. Many breakthrough products and services are born from a founder's gut feeling that there is an unmet need or a gap in the market, even when the data doesn't immediately support it. These founders are willing to take risks based on their intuition, confident that they are tapping into something that others haven't yet recognised. This boldness allows founder-led companies to innovate more aggressively than their competitors, often leading to significant market disruptions.

Ingvar Kamprad, founder of IKEA, provides a clear example of how instinct can drive innovation in founder mode. When Kamprad started IKEA, he had an instinctual belief that consumers would prefer affordable, flat-pack furniture that they could assemble themselves. At the time, data on the global furniture market suggested that consumers favoured pre-assembled, high-quality products. However, Kamprad's intuition about consumer behaviour proved correct, and IKEA revolutionised the furniture industry with its focus on low-cost, do-it-yourself products. By trusting his instincts, Kamprad created one of the most successful and innovative retail companies in the world.

Balancing Instinct with Experience

While instinct is a powerful tool in founder mode, it doesn't operate in isolation. Successful founders often combine their instincts with experience and expertise in their industry. Over time, founders develop a deep understanding of their markets, customers, and competitors, which sharpens their intuition and helps them make better decisions. The most effective instinctual decisions are those that are informed by years of learning, observation, and hands-on experience.

Sophia Amoruso, founder of Nasty Gal, used her instincts to turn a small eBay vintage clothing store into a multimillion-dollar fashion brand. Amoruso's success was driven by her ability to spot fashion trends early and curate unique products that appealed to a growing online audience of young women. Even before data could confirm her customers' preferences, Amoruso trusted her intuition about what would sell. Over time, her instincts were refined by her growing knowledge of the fashion industry and her direct interactions with her customer base. While Nasty Gal eventually faced challenges as it scaled, Amoruso's early success underscores the importance of instinct combined with experience in creating a brand that resonated with its target market.

Founders who balance instinct with experience can also better navigate the risks associated with gut-based decision-making. Instinct can sometimes lead to costly mistakes if it isn't tempered by practical knowledge. For example, a founder who has a strong instinct about a new product idea may be able to avoid common pitfalls in execution if they draw on their prior experience in product development or market testing. This combination of instinct and expertise allows founders to make more informed, confident decisions.

When Instinct Goes Against the Grain

Founders trust their instincts even when it means defying expert advice or industry norms. While this approach carries risk, it can also lead to significant breakthroughs, as founders who follow their intuition often see opportunities that others miss.

Anita Roddick, founder of The Body Shop, trusted her instincts to create a brand built on ethical consumerism and natural beauty products, long before sustainability and corporate social responsibility became mainstream values in the beauty industry. In the early years of The Body Shop, market research suggested that consumers preferred traditional, luxury beauty products, and there was little data to support the idea that environmentally friendly, cruelty-free products could compete. However, Roddick's instinct told her that consumers were ready for a change, and she built The Body Shop around her belief in natural ingredients, fair trade, and ethical practices. Her instincts proved right, and The Body Shop became a pioneering brand in the beauty industry, paving the way for the growing demand for sustainable products.

How Founders Can Strengthen Their Instincts Over Time

While many founders are celebrated for their natural instincts, these gut feelings don't emerge in a vacuum. Successful founders continuously develop and refine their instincts through experience, self-reflection, learning from mistakes, and staying in tune with their market and industry.

One of the most important ways founders can strengthen their instincts is by gaining hands-on experience and reflecting on past decisions. Founders who have been through various stages of building, scaling, and managing a company naturally develop stronger instincts, as each decision they make adds to their knowledge base. However, experience alone is not enough; founders must actively reflect on their past decisions—whether they led to success or failure—to draw insights that will shape their future instincts.

Reflective practice helps founders understand why certain decisions worked and why others didn't, allowing them to refine their gut instincts. Taking the time to evaluate the outcomes of key decisions can reveal patterns or blind spots in their decision-making process, enabling them to trust their instincts more confidently the next time they face a similar situation.

Instincts often become sharper when founders push themselves outside their comfort zones and take calculated risks. Risk-taking, especially in early-stage companies, is a necessary part of founder mode, and it's through these risks that founders develop a stronger sense of intuition. Every risk, whether it leads to success or failure, provides new data points that founders can use to refine their decision-making process.

Failure, in particular, is a powerful teacher for founders looking to strengthen their instincts. When founders take risks and fail, they are forced to confront the reasons why their instincts may have led them astray, allowing them to recalibrate and make more informed decisions in the future. Instead of viewing failure as a setback, founders can treat it as an opportunity to learn and adjust, building a more resilient and adaptive decision-making framework.

Evan Williams, co-founder of Twitter and Medium, has embraced risk-taking throughout his career. Before finding success with Twitter, Williams faced several failures, including his earlier venture Odeo, which aimed to create a podcasting platform. When Apple launched iTunes with podcasting features, Odeo's business model became obsolete. Williams learned from this failure and pivoted, trusting his instincts to pursue a new idea that eventually led to Twitter. The failure of Odeo helped Williams strengthen his instincts about market timing, product development, and the importance of focusing on user needs, which contributed to his later success.

Instincts can be sharpened by striking the right balance between gut feelings and data-driven insights. While founders may rely heavily on their instincts, especially in uncertain or ambiguous situations, they can also use data as a tool to either confirm or challenge their initial intuition. This balance allows founders to make more informed decisions without becoming overly dependent on data or second-guessing their instincts.

Data can provide important context and validation for instinctual decisions, helping founders identify trends, customer preferences, or operational efficiencies that align with their gut feelings. However, founders must also recognise when data is incomplete or potentially misleading, especially in new markets or innovative industries where traditional metrics may not capture the full picture.

Founders who want to sharpen their instincts must stay deeply connected to their market, customers, and industry trends. The best instincts are often rooted in a strong understanding of the customer's needs and behaviours, and founders who actively engage with their target audience can develop a more intuitive sense of how to serve them. This close connection to the market allows founders to anticipate shifts, spot new opportunities, and adapt quickly, even when the data doesn't point clearly in one direction.

Founders who distance themselves from their customers or industry as they scale risk losing touch with the instincts that originally drove their success. By regularly interacting with customers, participating in industry events, and staying curious about emerging trends, founders can keep their instincts sharp and continue making decisions that align with their company's mission and market needs.

Richard Reed, co-founder of Innocent Drinks, is known for staying close to his customers. When Innocent was in its early stages, Reed and his team used creative methods to engage directly with customers, including setting up a stall at a music festival to ask people if they liked the idea of healthy smoothies. By maintaining this direct connection with his target audience, Reed developed a strong intuition about what products would resonate with consumers and how to market them effectively.

Chapter 6
Risk Tolerance: A Defining Factor in Founder Mode

One of the most striking differences between founders and managers lies in their approach to risk. Founders are often known for embracing risk in ways that would be uncomfortable—or even unacceptable—in traditional management roles. While managers are typically tasked with maintaining stability, minimising risk, and focusing on short-term operational success, founders are more likely to take significant risks in pursuit of long-term vision and innovation. This risk-tolerant behaviour is a defining characteristic of founder mode and is often critical to a company's ability to disrupt industries, create new markets, and achieve breakthrough innovations.

In this chapter, we will explore how founders embrace risk differently from managers and why this behaviour is essential to driving innovation. We will examine the mindset behind risk tolerance in founder mode, why it enables founders to push boundaries, and how it allows them to lead their companies through periods of uncertainty and volatility.

The Risk-Tolerant Mindset in Founder Mode

Risk tolerance is deeply embedded in the mindset of founders, who are often driven by a strong belief in their vision and a willingness to take significant chances to bring that vision to life. Founders, after all, are tasked with creating something entirely new. This act of creation —whether it's a new product, service, or business model—requires a high degree of risk tolerance, as the path forward is often unclear, untested, and fraught with potential failure.

For founders, the prospect of failure is not a deterrent but rather a natural part of the entrepreneurial process. Founders understand that innovation involves trial and error, and they are often willing to experiment, pivot, and iterate on their ideas, knowing that success may only come after a series of failures. This willingness to take risks and embrace uncertainty enables founders to explore new opportunities that others might avoid, leading to groundbreaking innovations and new markets.

Why Founders Embrace Risk: The Connection to Innovation

Risk tolerance is not only a personality trait but also a strategic approach that is essential to fostering innovation. Founders who are willing to take risks create environments where experimentation is encouraged, and bold ideas can flourish. This is critical in industries undergoing disruption or where the future is uncertain, as traditional management practices focused on minimising risk can lead to stagnation and missed opportunities.

The relationship between risk and innovation is particularly evident in the early stages of a company, where founders must make decisions without the benefit of clear data or proven models. These decisions often involve high levels of uncertainty—whether it's launching a new product, entering a new market, or adopting a novel technology. Founders who are risk-tolerant are more likely to make the leap, while risk-averse leaders may hesitate, waiting for more information or a safer option. However, in fast-moving industries, waiting too long can result in missed opportunities or falling behind competitors.

Strategies for Managing Risk While Maintaining Innovation

While embracing risk is essential to founder mode, the most successful founders don't simply take risks blindly—they employ strategies to manage and mitigate those risks while maintaining a culture of innovation. The challenge for founders is to find a balance between bold decision-making and thoughtful risk management, ensuring that their company can innovate without exposing itself to unnecessary dangers.

Calculated Risk-Taking: Know When to Leap and When to Hold Back

Founders need to be able to discern when a risk is worth taking and when it may lead to catastrophic failure. The most successful founders are not reckless; they are strategic, choosing their battles and making sure that the potential upside of a risk outweighs the potential downside.

A calculated risk involves gathering as much information as possible to make an informed decision while accepting that there will always be some uncertainty. Founders should evaluate factors such as market demand, potential competition, technological feasibility, and financial impact before making high-stakes decisions. However, it's also important not to get paralysed by analysis—there will never be perfect information, and founders must be willing to act decisively when the time is right.

Creating a Culture That Encourages Smart Risk-Taking

Founders who want to maintain a culture of innovation must foster an environment where smart risk-taking is encouraged. Innovation thrives when employees feel empowered to take risks, experiment with new ideas, and pursue creative solutions without fear of failure. However—there must be a framework in place that promotes thoughtful risk-taking aligned with the company's goals.

One way to create this culture is by celebrating both successes and failures as part of the innovation process. When failures occur, they should be viewed as learning opportunities, not punishable offences. Employees should be encouraged to take risks as long as they are calculated and aligned with the company's mission. By promoting a mindset where failure is a natural part of growth, founders can inspire their teams to push boundaries and explore new opportunities.

Using Pilot Programmes and Prototypes to Test Ideas

One effective way for founders to manage risk is by using pilot programmes and prototyping to test new ideas on a smaller scale before fully committing. By starting with a limited rollout or creating a prototype, founders can experiment with new products, services, or strategies without incurring the full cost or risk of a company-wide launch. This approach allows for rapid iteration and testing, providing valuable feedback that can help improve the idea before it is scaled up.

Pilot programmes and prototypes are especially useful in industries with high levels of uncertainty or where consumer preferences can change quickly. By collecting real-world data from these smaller experiments, founders can make more informed decisions about whether to invest further or pivot in a new direction. This minimises the financial and operational risk associated with launching untested innovations while still allowing for bold experimentation.

Diversifying Risk

Another important strategy for managing risk while maintaining innovation is diversification. Founders can diversify risk by exploring multiple avenues for growth or innovation simultaneously, ensuring that the failure of one initiative doesn't threaten the entire company.

Diversification can take many forms, including product diversification, geographic expansion, or exploring new revenue streams.

By not relying on a single product or market for success, founders can spread risk across different parts of the business. This allows them to take bolder risks in one area while maintaining stability in others. Diversification also provides a buffer against market fluctuations, changes in consumer preferences, or competitive pressures, enabling founders to continue innovating even when facing uncertainty.

Building a Strong Support Network

Finally, founders can manage risk more effectively by building a strong support network of advisors, mentors, and investors. Having trusted advisors who can provide feedback, challenge assumptions, and offer expertise can help founders make more informed decisions and avoid potential pitfalls. A robust support network can also provide valuable resources and connections that can mitigate risk, such as access to funding, industry insights, or operational expertise.

By surrounding themselves with a diverse group of advisors who bring different perspectives, founders can avoid tunnel vision and gain a clearer understanding of the risks they're facing. This support network also helps founders make smarter decisions when it comes to balancing bold innovation with prudent risk management. Advisors and mentors can act as a sounding board for founders' ideas, providing a more objective analysis of the potential risks and benefits involved. This reduces the chances of overestimating the rewards or underestimating the challenges of pursuing high-risk ventures.

Additionally, investors and stakeholders play a crucial role in helping founders manage risk, particularly when it comes to securing the financial resources needed to support innovation. Having investors who believe in the long-term vision of the company and are willing to back high-risk projects is essential for enabling bold innovation. Founders should build relationships with investors who understand the nature of entrepreneurial risk and are willing to support experimentation, even if it doesn't always yield immediate returns.

Jon Smith

Evan Spiegel, co-founder of Snap Inc., surrounded himself with a network of advisors and mentors who helped guide him through the challenges of launching Snapchat in a highly competitive tech environment. Spiegel's ability to take calculated risks, such as turning down a $3 billion acquisition offer from Facebook in 2013, was bolstered by the advice and support of those around him. This network helped him navigate the risks of scaling Snapchat, enabling the company to grow into one of the most influential social media platforms despite the initial scepticism of many investors and competitors.

Chapter 7
Customer Obsession as a Core Principle

In founder-led companies, one of the most critical elements of success is often a deep, unwavering focus on customers. This commitment, often referred to as "customer obsession," goes beyond merely satisfying customer needs—founders in customer-obsessed companies build their entire businesses around creating exceptional experiences for their customers. By staying intimately connected to customer feedback, founders are able to understand their customers' pain points and preferences on a granular level, allowing them to create products and services that resonate deeply with their target market.

In this chapter, we will explore the role of customer obsession as a core principle in founder mode, examining how founders' direct involvement in customer feedback has led to breakthrough innovations and sustained growth. Through case studies of companies where customer feedback has been pivotal in driving product development, we'll highlight the benefits of staying customer-centric throughout a company's lifecycle.

Customer Obsession: Beyond Meeting Needs

At its core, customer obsession means going beyond simply meeting customer needs and instead seeking to delight and surprise customers in ways they didn't even expect. Founders who adopt a customer-obsessed mindset are relentless in their pursuit of understanding what their customers truly want, often spending time engaging directly with them to gather insights that drive product decisions. This type of involvement can be especially powerful in the early stages of a company when customer feedback helps refine product offerings and steer the company's growth trajectory.

Unlike traditional companies that may rely heavily on market research or surveys, founders in customer-obsessed companies often take a hands-on approach, frequently interacting with customers to understand their needs on a personal level. This deep connection to customers helps founders anticipate changes in demand, identify untapped opportunities, and ensure that their products remain relevant and useful as the company grows.

Key components of customer obsession in founder mode:

- **Deep engagement with customers**: Founders who prioritise customer obsession often interact with customers directly, using feedback to inform key decisions.
- **Proactive problem-solving**: Customer-obsessed founders don't wait for customers to voice concerns—they anticipate issues and address them before they become problems.
- **Focus on long-term customer loyalty**: Rather than simply aiming for transactional success, customer-obsessed founders work to create lasting relationships with customers, leading to loyalty and sustained growth.

The Founder's Role in Customer Feedback and Product Breakthroughs

Founders who are closely involved in gathering and responding to customer feedback are often able to drive breakthrough innovations. This is because they are uniquely positioned to act quickly on the insights they gather, iterating on their products or services, in near-real-time to better meet customer needs. Founders who remain engaged with customers throughout the product development process can identify features or improvements that may not be immediately obvious from market data alone.

Ben Silbermann, co-founder of Pinterest, exemplified how direct involvement with customers can lead to significant product breakthroughs. When Pinterest was in its early stages, Silbermann personally reached out to users, emailing and calling them to gather feedback about their experience with the platform. This engagement gave him invaluable insights into how users were interacting with Pinterest, which features they loved, and where they were encountering difficulties. Based on this feedback, Silbermann and his team made numerous adjustments to the product's design and functionality, which helped Pinterest grow from a niche service into a globally popular platform. Silbermann's obsession with understanding his users' behaviour allowed him to create a product that resonated deeply with people, turning Pinterest into a social media powerhouse.

Building a Culture of Customer Obsession

For customer obsession to be successful over the long term, founders need to instil this mindset across the entire organisation. As companies grow, it becomes increasingly difficult for founders to interact directly with every customer, so it's essential that customer-centric thinking is embedded in the company's culture. This means empowering employees at all levels to take ownership of the customer experience and encouraging them to act with the same level of commitment to customers as the founder.

One company that has successfully built a culture of customer obsession is Zappos, under the leadership of Tony Hsieh. Hsieh made customer service the core of Zappos' business model, even prioritising it over short-term profitability. He famously encouraged customer service representatives to spend as much time as needed on the phone with customers, even if it meant chatting for hours about unrelated topics. By building a company culture that prioritised customer happiness, Hsieh ensured that Zappos developed a loyal customer base that valued the brand's commitment to exceptional service. Zappos' willingness to go above and beyond for customers became a key differentiator in the competitive e-commerce market, driving the company's growth and success.

As a company grows, maintaining a customer-obsessed culture becomes more challenging but also more critical. In the early stages of a startup, founders are often directly involved in every aspect of the customer experience, allowing them to gather insights and make quick decisions based on customer feedback. However, as the company scales, the founder's ability to personally interact with every customer diminishes. To maintain customer obsession as the company grows, founders need to implement strategies that ensure customer-centricity remains at the core of the organisation.

Embedding Customer Obsession in the Company Culture

When customer focus becomes part of the organisation's DNA, it transcends the actions of any one individual, including the founder. This means that even as the company grows, every team and department remains aligned with the goal of delivering exceptional customer experiences.

To achieve this, founders need to clearly communicate the importance of customer obsession to their teams and reinforce it through the company's values, goals, and performance metrics. Employees should understand that the company's success is directly tied to its ability to meet and exceed customer expectations, and this should be reflected in hiring practices, training, and internal communications. Founders can lead by example, modelling customer-centric behaviours in their own decision-making and interactions with customers and employees alike.

Empowering Teams to Take Ownership of Customer Experience

As companies grow, founders must empower their teams to take ownership of the customer experience. This requires giving employees the autonomy to make decisions that improve customer satisfaction, whether it's solving a customer's problem, improving a product feature, or enhancing the overall user experience. When employees feel empowered to act in the customer's best interest, they are more likely to go above and beyond to ensure customer happiness.

Empowering teams also means providing them with the tools and resources they need to understand customer needs. This could involve regular training on customer empathy, giving teams access to customer feedback data, or creating cross-functional teams focused on improving the customer journey. Founders should encourage a culture where every employee, regardless of their department or role, sees themselves as a steward of the customer experience.

Leveraging Technology to Stay Connected to Customers

By using customer relationship management (CRM) tools, analytics platforms, and automation, companies can gather valuable insights about customer behaviour, preferences, and pain points at scale.

CRM tools allow companies to centralise customer data, making it easier for teams to track interactions, monitor customer satisfaction, and identify areas for improvement. Analytics platforms can provide real-time feedback on customer engagement, allowing companies to make data-driven decisions about product development, marketing, and customer service. Automation can also play a role in scaling customer support, enabling companies to handle routine inquiries efficiently while freeing up human agents to focus on more complex, personalised interactions.

While technology can't replace the personal touch of direct customer engagement, it can provide valuable insights that allow companies to maintain a high level of customer focus even as they grow. Founders should ensure that technology is used to complement, not replace, the company's human-centric approach to customer service.

Continuously Soliciting and Acting on Customer Feedback

Customer obsession is not a one-time effort—it requires continuous engagement with customers to understand their evolving needs and preferences. As companies grow, founders should establish processes for regularly soliciting and acting on customer feedback. This could involve regular customer surveys, focus groups, user testing, or social media monitoring. The key is to create multiple feedback loops that allow the company to stay in tune with customer sentiment at all times.

Once feedback is collected, it's important to act on it promptly. Companies should have mechanisms in place for prioritising customer feedback and making changes that improve the customer experience. Whether it's addressing a bug in the product, improving customer service processes, or launching a new feature based on user requests, companies that respond quickly to customer feedback build trust and loyalty.

SECTION TWO

Building and Scaling in Founder Mode

Chapter 8
Hiring in Founder Mode: What to Look for

Hiring is one of the most critical decisions that founders make, and it plays a pivotal role in shaping the future of a company. In founder mode, hiring decisions go beyond just finding candidates with the right technical skills; it's about identifying people who align with the founder's vision, values, and culture. While managers may prioritise operational efficiency and filling specific skill gaps, founders are more focused on building a team that will help bring their entrepreneurial vision to life. In this chapter, we will explore the nuances of hiring in founder mode, offering advice on how founders can find the right people who not only fit the technical requirements but also share the passion and drive needed to scale the business.

Hiring for Vision and Mission Alignment

Founders need to identify candidates who not only understand the vision but are excited about the opportunity to contribute to it. To ensure alignment with the company's vision, founders should focus on asking questions that explore a candidate's motivation and values. Instead of focusing solely on technical qualifications, founders should dive deeper into why candidates want to work for the company, how they perceive the company's mission, and what excites them about being part of a startup or entrepreneurial venture. This helps identify whether the candidate shares the same passion and enthusiasm for the company's goals.

Hiring for Cultural Fit

Founders should seek candidates who share the company's core values and can contribute positively to the existing culture. This doesn't mean hiring people who are identical in personality or background, but rather individuals who align with the company's principles and will thrive in its environment.

Hiring for cultural fit in founder mode often involves assessing how well candidates will adapt to the startup's pace, uncertainty, and collaborative style. In early-stage companies, flexibility, resilience, and adaptability are essential traits, as employees are often required to take on multiple roles, adjust to rapid changes, and contribute in creative ways. Founders should look for candidates who are comfortable with ambiguity, willing to take initiative, and able to work well in a fast-paced, entrepreneurial environment.

Hiring for Versatility and Resilience

In founder mode, startups often require employees to wear many hats and adapt to changing circumstances. Founders should prioritise candidates who can handle the unpredictable nature of startup life, thrive under pressure, and demonstrate a willingness to step outside of their job description to help the company succeed.

Founders need to assess whether candidates are comfortable with the fluidity of startup roles and whether they have the problem-solving skills to navigate challenges that arise as the company scales. Versatile employees are able to contribute across multiple functions, which is especially valuable in a resource-constrained startup environment where every team member plays a crucial role.

Differences Between Founder Mode and Manager Mode in Hiring

Manager mode tends to focus on stability and specialisation, while founder mode requires flexibility, passion, and a willingness to contribute to multiple areas of the business.

Key differences between hiring in founder mode and manager mode:

- **Vision-driven vs. role-driven**: In founder mode, hiring is driven by the company's long-term vision, while in manager mode, it's focused on filling specific roles and responsibilities.
- **Holistic assessment vs. technical fit**: Founder mode emphasises cultural fit, passion, and versatility, whereas manager mode prioritises technical skills and operational efficiency.
- **Entrepreneurial mindset vs. specialisation**: Founder mode looks for candidates with an entrepreneurial mindset who can contribute broadly, while manager mode seeks specialists for specific tasks.

Crafting an Interview Process that Identifies Mission-Driven Candidates

In founder mode, identifying candidates who are driven by the company's mission is essential. Founders need to ensure that new hires are not just there for a paycheck but are motivated by the opportunity to contribute to something larger than themselves. An interview process that prioritises mission alignment will help founders find people who are genuinely excited about the company's purpose and vision, ensuring long-term engagement and dedication.

Designing an Onboarding Process that Reinforces Mission and Culture

Hiring in founder mode doesn't end when a candidate accepts the offer—it extends into how they are onboarded and integrated into the company. A strong onboarding process is essential for reinforcing the company's mission, culture, and values from day one. Onboarding is an opportunity to ensure that new hires understand the company's vision and feel connected to its purpose.

Founders should design an onboarding programme that emphasises the company's mission and culture. This might include sessions where the founder or senior leaders share the company's story, explain its long-term goals, and highlight the values that guide everyday decision-making. Providing context around the company's purpose helps new employees see how their role contributes to the bigger picture.

To help new hires acclimate to the company's culture, founders can create opportunities for them to engage with other employees through team-building activities, mentorship programmes, and informal meetings. Encouraging interaction across different teams helps reinforce the collaborative and mission-focused culture of the company.

As startups experience rapid growth, the pressure to hire quickly can lead to mistakes that have long-lasting effects on the company's culture and performance. In founder mode, where the early team is crucial to shaping the trajectory of the business, rushing the hiring process or prioritising immediate needs over long-term alignment can be detrimental. Founders must be mindful of the common hazards that arise during periods of rapid expansion and implement strategies to avoid them.

Chapter 9
The Challenges of Delegation

Delegation is one of the most difficult skills for many founders to master, yet it is also one of the most crucial for scaling a company. However, letting go of control is easier said than done. Many founders struggle with delegation due to psychological, emotional, and strategic reasons, which can lead to burnout, bottlenecks, and stalled growth.

In this chapter, we will explore why delegation is so challenging for founders, examining the psychological and strategic factors that make it difficult. We will also provide practical strategies for overcoming these challenges, enabling founders to delegate effectively and build a strong, self-sufficient team that can drive the company forward.

Why Founders Struggle with Delegation

Founders are deeply connected to their companies, and the thought of handing over responsibility to others can be daunting. Below, we explore the main reasons why founders find it hard to delegate and how these challenges manifest in a growing business.

Founders typically feel a deep sense of ownership and emotional attachment to their companies. After all, they've invested significant time, energy, and resources into building their business from the ground up. This personal connection can make it difficult to trust others with key decisions and tasks, as founders often feel that no one else understands the company's vision, values, or nuances as well as they do.

Founders who are highly attached to their business may feel that delegating tasks means relinquishing control or compromising the quality of work. They may worry that others won't approach tasks with the same level of care, attention to detail, or commitment to the company's success. This psychological ownership can lead to micro-management, where founders remain overly involved in day-to-day operations, even when delegation would be more effective.

When delegating tasks, consider how they can serve as growth opportunities for your team members. Assign projects that challenge employees to step outside their comfort zones and develop new skills. Provide guidance and support along the way, but allow them to take ownership of the task and begin to build their own psychological connection to the business, beyond the transactional nature of simply being employed. This not only helps employees grow but also builds a more capable leadership team for the future.

Fear of Losing Control

In the early stages of a startup, founders often have a hands-on role in every decision and process, which gives them a sense of control over the company's direction. As the business grows and becomes more complex, it's impossible for one person to manage everything, but the fear of losing control can prevent founders from delegating tasks to others.

Founders who fear losing control may hesitate to delegate because they worry that others won't make the same decisions they would. This fear can lead to over-involvement, where founders feel the need to oversee every aspect of the business, even when it's no longer necessary or sustainable. This approach can create bottle-necks, as team members become dependent on the founder's approval for even minor decisions, slowing down progress and innovation.

Clearly outline the scope of each team member's decision-making authority. When team members understand what decisions they can make on their own and which ones require input from leadership, it reduces uncertainty and gives them the confidence to act autonomously. No one likes ambiguity and therefore, this also helps founders feel more comfortable with delegation, knowing that major decisions will still involve their input.

Regular check-ins and reporting structures allow founders to stay informed about the progress of delegated tasks without having to micromanage. By setting up a regular cadence for updates—whether through meetings, dashboards, or written reports—founders can monitor key performance indicators (KPIs) and intervene only when necessary.

Clearly outline the scope of each team member's decision-making authority. When team members understand what decisions they can make on their own and which ones require input from leadership, it reduces uncertainty and gives them the confidence to act autonomously. This also helps founders feel more comfortable with delegation, knowing that major decisions will still involve their input.

Perfectionism and High Standards

Many founders are perfectionists who set extremely high standards for themselves and their teams. While this drive for excellence can be a strength, it can also make it difficult for founders to trust others to handle tasks to the same level of quality, leading them to take on more work than is sustainable.

Perfectionism often leads to micromanagement, as founders may feel compelled to oversee every detail of a project to ensure it meets their standards. This not only places an unsustainable workload on the founder but also stifles the development of team members, who are unable to take ownership of their work. Perfectionist founders may also struggle to accept that mistakes or imperfections are part of the learning process for their team.

One of the hardest things for perfectionists to accept is that mistakes are part of the growth process. Founders need to understand that team members won't always execute tasks exactly as they would, but that doesn't mean the work won't be done well. By giving employees the opportunity to learn from their mistakes, founders foster a culture of growth and improvement.

Founders should focus on the results they want to achieve rather than the exact methods their teams use to get there. By allowing team members the freedom to find their own way of solving problems, founders empower them to take ownership of their work. This shift in focus from process to outcomes helps reduce the founder's tendency to micromanage while still ensuring that key goals are met.

Lack of Trust in Others

A lack of trust in their team members to handle important tasks can stem from a variety of sources, including previous experiences where delegation didn't go as planned, a fear of failure, or simply the founder's belief that they are the only one who truly understands the company's needs.

In the long run, a lack of trust can lead to burnout for the founder and disengagement among employees who feel micromanaged. If trust is an issue, start delegating smaller, low-risk tasks to team members. This allows the founder to gradually build confidence in their team's abilities. As employees complete these tasks successfully, trust grows, and founders can feel more comfortable delegating larger and more important responsibilities.

Often, founders hesitate to delegate because they're unsure whether their team has the necessary skills to succeed. Investing in training and development ensures that team members have the knowledge and tools they need to perform their roles effectively. This also gives founders peace of mind, knowing that their team is well-prepared to handle delegated tasks and better qualified in general.

Chapter 10
Structuring an Organisation in Founder Mode

In founder-led companies, the organisational structure plays a pivotal role in maintaining the founder's vision while enabling the company to scale effectively. The way a company is structured directly influences decision-making processes, communication flows, and how aligned employees remain with the company's mission. In founder mode, where the founder's influence is often central to the company's growth, choosing the right structure is essential for balancing the need for autonomy and innovation with the need for oversight and direction.

In this chapter, we'll discuss how organisational structures can be shaped to support founder-driven leadership. We'll explore the key differences between flat and hierarchical structures, the advantages and challenges of each, and how founders can design an organisation that sustains both innovation and operational efficiency.

The Role of Organisational Structure in Founder Mode

A company's organisational structure defines how tasks are assigned, who reports to whom, and how decisions are made. In founder mode, the structure must support the founder's leadership style, providing enough flexibility to maintain innovation while ensuring that teams are aligned with the company's long-term vision.

Flat vs. Hierarchical Structures in Founder-Led Companies

When structuring a company in founder mode, one of the key decisions is whether to adopt a flat or hierarchical structure. Both models offer distinct advantages and challenges, and the right choice depends on the company's size, industry, and growth stage.

Advantages of a Flat Structure in Founder Mode:

Agility and Speed: Flat structures enable faster decision-making, as there are fewer layers of management to go through. This is particularly beneficial in fast-paced industries or early-stage startups, where rapid iteration and quick responses to market changes are critical.

Close Connection to the Founder: In a flat structure, employees often have direct access to the founder, which helps maintain alignment with the company's vision and values. The founder can provide real-time feedback, influence key decisions, and stay connected to the day-to-day activities of the business.

Innovation and Collaboration: Without rigid hierarchies, employees in a flat organisation are encouraged to share ideas, collaborate across departments, and experiment with new solutions. This fosters a culture of innovation, where teams feel empowered to contribute creatively to the company's growth.

Challenges of a Flat Structure in Founder Mode:

Scaling Complexity: While a flat structure works well in the early stages, it can become difficult to manage as the company scales. With limited layers of management, the founder may become overwhelmed with the number of direct reports and decisions they need to oversee. This can lead to bottlenecks and reduced efficiency as the organisation grows.

Lack of Clear Career Progression: In a flat structure, employees may struggle to see a clear path for career advancement. Without traditional management levels, it can be difficult for employees to envision how they can grow within the company, leading to potential disengagement or turnover.

Potential for Over-Involvement: In founder-led companies, a flat structure can lead to over-involvement from the founder. With direct access to the founder, employees may rely too heavily on their input, leading to decision-making bottlenecks and limiting team autonomy.

Valve Corporation, a video game development company, operates with a flat organisational structure. The company is known for its lack of formal management hierarchy, where employees are free to work on projects of their choosing. This structure fosters a culture of creativity and innovation, allowing Valve to produce groundbreaking games like *Half-Life* and *Portal*. However, as Valve grew, the flat structure also led to challenges in coordination and long-term project management, highlighting some of the difficulties of scaling with a flat approach.

Blending Flat and Hierarchical Structures in Founder-Led Companies

While flat and hierarchical organisational structures each offer distinct advantages and challenges, many founder-led companies find success by adopting a hybrid approach that blends the best elements of both. This hybrid structure allows companies to maintain agility and innovation at the lower levels, where teams need the flexibility to experiment and iterate, while establishing clear oversight and control at the upper levels to ensure alignment with the company's mission and strategic goals.

The Need for Balance in Founder Mode

A purely flat structure may work in the early stages of a startup, but as the company scales, it can create bottlenecks and reduce efficiency. On the other hand, a strictly hierarchical structure might stifle innovation and create barriers between employees and the founder.

By blending elements of both structures, founders can maintain direct influence over strategic decisions while allowing teams to work autonomously. This hybrid approach enables the company to stay nimble and responsive to market changes while scaling operations in a controlled and efficient manner.

While strategic oversight is centralised at the top, a hybrid structure allows for greater autonomy and flexibility at the lower levels of the organisation. Teams are empowered to make decisions, experiment with new ideas, and respond quickly to changes in the market without needing constant approval from upper management. This autonomy encourages a culture of innovation and ownership, where employees feel trusted to take risks, get stuff done, and drive the company forward. One way to achieve this is through skip-level engagement covered in the next chapter.

Chapter 11
The Importance of Skip-Level Engagement

Skip-level engagement is an essential tool for founders looking to stay connected with their organisation as it scales. As companies grow, founders inevitably become more removed from the day-to-day operations, making it harder to maintain direct relationships with employees and ensure alignment with the company's vision. Skip-level meetings provide a structured way for founders to engage with employees who report to their direct reports, enabling them to stay in touch with the pulse of the organisation, identify potential issues early, and reinforce company culture.

In this chapter, we'll explore the concept of skip-level meetings in detail, why they're critical for founders, and how they can strengthen organisational culture and drive innovation. We'll also look at actionable strategies for implementing skip-level engagement effectively within your organisation.

What Are Skip-Level Meetings?

A skip-level meeting is a meeting in which senior leaders, including founders, meet directly with employees who are at least one level below their direct reports, effectively "skipping" the middle manage-ment layer. These meetings are an opportunity for senior leaders to get unfiltered feedback from the people who are on the front lines of the business—those who are closest to the customers, products, and daily operations.

Skip-level meetings differ from traditional leadership meetings in that they bypass the direct chain of command, allowing founders to hear directly from employees without the filter of their managers. This provides a more nuanced and ground-level view of the organisa-tion, helping leaders understand what's really happening at every level of the company.

Founders often face the challenge of losing touch with the reality of their company as it grows, especially as layers of management are added. Skip-level meetings help close this gap, providing valuable insights that might otherwise get lost in the hierarchy. These meet-ings also give employees a chance to connect with senior leadership, fostering a culture of openness and inclusion.

Jeff Bezos at Amazon famously used skip-level meetings to stay connected with his employees, even as Amazon grew into a global giant. Bezos regularly met with employees across various levels of the organisation to gain insights into operational challenges, customer feedback, and new ideas for products or features. These meetings helped Bezos remain informed about what was happening across the company and enabled him to identify opportunities for improvement and innovation that might not have been visible at the executive level.

Why Skip-Level Meetings Are Critical for Founders

- **Maintaining a Direct Connection to the Front Lines**: Skip-level meetings help founders stay connected to the employees who are executing the company's vision on the ground. These employees often have valuable insights into customer needs, product performance, and operational challenges that may not always reach senior leadership through traditional reporting structures.

- **Identifying Emerging Issues Early**: By engaging with employees at lower levels, founders can identify potential issues before they escalate. Employees may be more willing to share concerns or challenges in a skip-level meeting than they would in a formal report to their manager, making these meetings a valuable tool for early detection of problems.
- **Ensuring Alignment with the Company's Mission and Values**: As companies grow, there is a risk that different parts of the organisation may drift away from the core mission and values that the founder established. Skip-level meetings give founders the opportunity to reinforce the company's purpose and ensure that employees at every level are aligned with the overall vision.
- **Boosting Employee Morale and Engagement**: When employees feel heard by senior leadership, it boosts their morale and engagement. Skip-level meetings show employees that their voices matter and that their contributions are recognised by the founder and the company's leaders. This can have a positive impact on retention, productivity, and overall job satisfaction.

Indra Nooyi, former CEO of PepsiCo, regularly conducted skip-level meetings to stay connected with employees at all levels of the company. Nooyi's approach helped her understand the challenges and opportunities facing employees in different regions and functions. This direct engagement allowed her to keep a finger on the pulse across the global enterprise and make more informed decisions and reinforce PepsiCo's culture of collaboration and innovation.

Encouraging Grassroots Innovation

Frontline employees witness firsthand what works, what doesn't, and what could be done better. They should always be the first port of call when trying to measure the temperature of your customers or the market. Skip-level meetings provide a platform for these employees to share their insights directly with senior leadership, enabling them to propose innovative solutions to everyday challenges.

At Siemens, innovation is deeply embedded in the company culture through its 'Innovation Ecosystem.' Employees are encouraged to propose and develop new ideas via internal startup competitions, hackathons, and cross-functional innovation teams. Siemens' 'Picture of the Future' programme invites employees from all levels to envision and develop forward-thinking projects, some of which have become key advancements in sectors like energy, automation, and transportation. By empowering grassroots innovation, Siemens has maintained its leadership in the industrial technology space.

Nurturing a Culture of Continuous Improvement

Skip-level meetings are also an excellent way for founders to nurture a culture of continuous improvement. By regularly engaging with employees at different levels of the organisation, founders signal that the company is always open to new ideas and that innovation is not limited to the C-suite. This creates a feedback loop where employees feel encouraged to continually look for ways to improve processes, products, and services, knowing that their suggestions will be heard by senior leadership.

Toyota, through its famous Kaizen philosophy of continuous improvement, has long encouraged employees at all levels to suggest process improvements. While Kaizen is embedded in Toyota's culture, skip-level engagement plays a role in ensuring that feedback from employees on the factory floor reaches senior leadership. This ongoing dialogue has led to countless innovations in Toyota's production processes, resulting in more efficient operations and higher-quality products.

Best Practices for Conducting Effective Skip-Level Meetings

While skip-level meetings offer tremendous value for maintaining a founder's influence and driving innovation, their success depends on how effectively they are conducted. If skip-level meetings are poorly structured or if employees don't feel comfortable sharing candid feedback, these meetings can become superficial, failing to yield meaningful insights. Founders must approach skip-level meetings with intentionality, creating an environment where employees feel empowered to speak openly and where actionable outcomes are the focus.

1. Set Clear Objectives for Each Meeting

For skip-level meetings to be effective, it's important to approach them with clear objectives in mind. Founders should decide in advance what they hope to achieve from each meeting, whether it's gathering feedback on a specific initiative, understanding employee pain points, or fostering a stronger connection with frontline workers.

Without a specific purpose, skip-level meetings can become unfocused or feel like a formality rather than a genuine opportunity for dialogue. By setting clear objectives, founders can steer the conversation in a direction that generates valuable insights while ensuring that the time spent is productive for both parties.

2. Foster an Atmosphere of Trust and Openness

The success of skip-level meetings hinges on whether employees feel comfortable sharing honest feedback with senior leadership. If employees fear retribution for speaking candidly, or if they feel that their input won't be taken seriously, these meetings will not be effective. Founders must work to create an atmosphere of trust, where employees feel safe sharing their thoughts, concerns, and ideas without fear of judgment.

Founders should approach these meetings with humility and a genuine curiosity to learn from employees. It's important to reassure employees that the meeting is a safe space for open dialogue and that their feedback is valued. Listening without interruption, avoiding defensiveness, and thanking employees for their input are all critical for building trust in these meetings.

3. Keep Meetings Focused and Time-Efficient

While it's important for skip-level meetings to be open-ended in terms of discussion topics, it's equally crucial to keep them focused and time-efficient. Founders' schedules are often packed, and employees are also busy with their day-to-day responsibilities, so meetings that drag on without clear direction can feel unproductive. The key is to balance open dialogue with a structured approach to ensure that the meeting stays on track.

Founders should outline a basic structure for the meeting, including key topics to cover, and allocate time for each. For example, the first part of the meeting could be dedicated to hearing employee feedback, followed by a discussion on any specific initiatives or challenges the founder wants to address. Leaving time at the end for questions or open discussion ensures that important topics are covered without the meeting running too long. Each and every meeting is, of course, an opportunity to reinforce the founder's vision, and reinforce how that employee's role contributes to turning that vision into reality.

4. Follow Up on Actionable Outcomes

One of the biggest risks with skip-level meetings is that they can turn into an "inconsequential chat," where ideas are discussed but not acted upon. To prevent this, founders must follow up on actionable outcomes after the meeting. This shows employees that their feedback is being taken seriously and builds trust that skip-level meetings lead to tangible results.

After a skip-level meeting, founders should identify the key takeaways and decide which suggestions or concerns warrant further action. It's important to communicate the outcomes of the meeting back to the employees involved, whether it's through an email summarising the discussion or by implementing specific changes that were suggested. Even if certain suggestions can't be acted upon immediately, providing an explanation helps maintain transparency. Lastly, be it through the company's internal digital communication tools or quarterly/annual "all hands", initiatives, improvements, new products or features that were borne from skip-level meetings should be highlighted and celebrated company-wide.

5. Make Skip-Level Meetings a Regular Practice

For skip-level meetings to have a lasting impact, they need to become a regular part of the organisation's culture, not just a one-off event. Regular engagement helps maintain open lines of communication between founders and employees, ensuring that feedback continues to flow and that employees feel consistently connected to leadership.

Founders should schedule skip-level meetings with a wide variety of staff from different departments, and at a range of levels, at regular intervals, whether it's quarterly, bi-annually, or annually, depending on the size and needs of the organisation. Consistency is key to building trust and ensuring that these meetings become an integral part of the company's culture.

Chapter 12
Founder vs. Professional CEO: Lessons from the Trenches

One of the most pivotal decisions in the life cycle of a company is whether the founder should step aside and hand over the reins to a professional CEO. This decision can be fraught with challenges, emotions, and complex considerations. For some companies, bringing in an external CEO can lead to greater operational efficiency, scalability, and success. For others, the shift away from founder-led leadership results in the company losing its core identity, culture, or innovative edge. Understanding how and when to make this transition—and the potential consequences—is key for companies seeking to scale while maintaining their founding principles.

In this chapter, we will analyse real-world examples of companies where founders stepped aside for professional CEOs, the impact this change had on their success or failure, and the key lessons that can be drawn from these transitions.

Why Founders Step Aside

The decision for a founder to step aside often arises as the company grows beyond the skill set or interests of the original leader. Founders are typically visionaries who excel in the early stages of the business, but as the company scales, managing the complexities of day-to-day operations can become overwhelming. In other cases, the demands of shareholders or the board may push for a professional CEO with a different set of skills, particularly in areas like finance, logistics, or scaling operations. This transition can be strategic, but it often comes with significant risks.

Some key reasons founders step aside include:

- **Scaling challenges**: The company has grown so large that operational efficiency, supply chain management, and financial oversight require specialised expertise beyond what the founder may possess.
- **Investor or board pressure**: Investors or the board may push for a change in leadership to maximise shareholder value, especially in publicly traded companies.
- **Burnout or personal priorities**: Some founders step aside to avoid burnout or to pursue other ventures, such as launching new startups or philanthropic endeavours.
- **Transition to a strategic role**: Many founders shift to a chairman or advisory role, allowing them to focus on the vision and strategy of the company without being involved in the day-to-day operations.

Google is a well-known example where founders stepped aside for professional leadership. In 2001, co-founders Larry Page and Sergey Brin brought in Eric Schmidt as CEO to help scale the company. While Page and Brin were brilliant technologists, they recognised that the operational and business challenges of a rapidly growing company like Google required a more experienced executive. Schmidt's tenure as CEO allowed Google to scale its operations while maintaining the founders' vision and culture, making the transition a largely successful one.

Success Stories: When Professional CEOs Work

In some cases, the transition from a founder-led company to one led by a professional CEO can lead to significant success. Professional CEOs often bring the operational expertise, experience in scaling, and business acumen necessary to drive a company to the next level. Below are several examples where professional CEOs have taken founder-led companies to new heights.

Apple: Steve Jobs and Tim Cook

Perhaps one of the most famous examples of a successful founder-to-CEO transition is Apple. After Steve Jobs was forced out of Apple in 1985, the company struggled under a series of professional CEOs until Jobs was brought back in 1997. When Jobs returned, Apple was on the verge of bankruptcy. Jobs spearheaded a remarkable turnaround, focusing on innovation and product design to re-establish Apple's identity.

However, as the company grew, the operational demands became more complex. In 2011, as Jobs' health declined, he handpicked Tim Cook to succeed him as CEO. Cook, who had served as Apple's Chief Operating Officer, was not known for his visionary leadership but for his operational brilliance. Under Cook's leadership, Apple has grown into the most valuable company in the world, largely due to his expertise in managing supply chains, scaling operations, and expanding Apple's product lineup. While Cook's style differs from Jobs, Apple's transition is widely regarded as a success because Cook maintained the company's culture of innovation while focusing on operational excellence.

Microsoft: Bill Gates and Satya Nadella

Another compelling example is Microsoft. Founder Bill Gates stepped down as CEO in 2000, passing the torch to Steve Ballmer, who led the company for over a decade. Ballmer's tenure had its highs and lows—while Microsoft continued to generate profits, it missed key trends like mobile and cloud computing.

In 2014, Microsoft appointed Satya Nadella as CEO, and the

results have been transformational. Nadella refocused the company on cloud computing, AI, and subscription-based software, steering Microsoft away from its reliance on the Windows operating system. Under his leadership, Microsoft has seen explosive growth, with its market capitalisation more than tripling during his tenure. Nadella's success is often attributed to his ability to maintain Microsoft's engineering-driven culture while executing a new, forward-thinking vision.

Starbucks: Howard Schultz and Kevin Johnson

After decades of leading Starbucks, founder Howard Schultz handed over the reins to Kevin Johnson in 2017. Johnson, a former tech executive, had served as COO and was well-versed in Starbucks' operations and culture. Under Johnson's leadership, Starbucks expanded its global footprint, embraced digital transformation, and navigated challenging market dynamics, including the COVID-19 pandemic.

One of the reasons for this successful transition was that Johnson worked closely with Schultz for years before stepping into the CEO role, ensuring continuity in Starbucks' mission and culture. While Schultz had been the face of Starbucks' customer-centric and socially responsible brand, Johnson focused on scaling operations and improving the company's digital capabilities.

Whilst writing this book, it's been all change at Starbucks once again, following a startling reversal of fortune and slumping sales, with Brian Niccol appointed to the CEO role. Although it's too early to assess his impact on the business, it appears Niccol is taking a *founder mode* approach of going back to basics—by being transparent about the challenges the company faces and by spending more time 'on the shop floor' to reconnect the brand with staff and customers.

Failure Stories: When the Transition Doesn't Work

While there are many examples of successful transitions from founder to professional CEO, not all such changes lead to positive outcomes. In some cases, the introduction of a professional CEO leads to a loss of the company's identity or a misalignment with its core values, which can cause long-term damage. Below are some examples of failed transitions where founders stepped aside, only to watch their companies lose focus or struggle under new leadership.

Yahoo: Jerry Yang and Successive CEOs

Yahoo is a cautionary tale of what can happen when a company fails to find the right leadership after a founder steps aside. Jerry Yang, one of Yahoo's co-founders, served as CEO for a brief period, but the company struggled to maintain its position in the evolving tech landscape. Over the years, Yahoo brought in several high-profile professional CEOs, including Carol Bartz, Scott Thompson, and Marissa Mayer. Despite their efforts, Yahoo never regained its dominance in search, advertising, or digital media, and ultimately sold its core assets to Verizon in 2016.

One of the key reasons for Yahoo's failure was the lack of a coherent vision and the constant change in leadership direction. The company struggled to balance innovation with operational efficiency, and each successive CEO had a different approach to fixing Yahoo's problems. As a result, Yahoo became a company without a clear identity or strategy.

eBay: Pierre Omidyar and John Donahoe

In 2008, Pierre Omidyar, founder of eBay, stepped aside as CEO, and John Donahoe took over. While eBay remained profitable, under Donahoe's leadership, the company failed to innovate and keep up with the competitive threats posed by Amazon. The company's focus shifted from its marketplace roots toward PayPal, eventually leading to the spinoff of PayPal into a separate company in 2015. Many critics argue that eBay's lack of focus during Donahoe's tenure caused the company to lose its competitive edge.

Key Lessons from Founder-to-CEO Transitions

The transition from a founder to a professional CEO can be one of the most challenging moments in a company's lifecycle. While some companies navigate this shift smoothly and grow stronger, others struggle and lose their footing. A successful transition often hinges on how well the company preserves its founding culture, how effectively the new CEO can balance innovation with operational rigour, and how involved the founder remains after stepping down from the CEO role.

1. Maintain the Founder's Vision and Culture

Many founder-led companies are built on strong values, a mission-driven purpose, and a unique approach to innovation. When professional CEOs take over, it's crucial that they preserve the essence of the company's culture while implementing the operational improvements needed for scaling.

The culture of a company, particularly one that has been nurtured by a founder, is often one of its most valuable assets. It shapes how employees work, how customers perceive the brand, and how the company makes decisions. If the new CEO does not fully understand or appreciate the company's culture, they risk alienating employees, disrupting workflows, and losing what made the company successful in the first place.

When Marissa Mayer took over as CEO of Yahoo, she struggled to connect with the company's culture and identity, contributing to Yahoo's continued decline. Mayer's aggressive management style and efforts to reinvent Yahoo came at the expense of the company's core strengths, leading to a disconnection between leadership and employees.

2. Balance Innovation with Operational Efficiency

Another key lesson from successful founder-to-CEO transitions is the need to strike a balance between preserving innovation and introducing operational rigour. Founders are often visionaries who thrive on creating new products, disrupting industries, and pushing boundaries. However, as companies grow, they require a more structured approach to operations, including supply chain management, financial planning, and human resources. Professional CEOs are often brought in to handle these complexities, but they must be careful not to stifle the company's innovative spirit in the process.

If a new CEO imposes too much structure and rigidity, the company can become risk-averse and lose its competitive edge. On the other hand, a lack of operational discipline can lead to inefficiencies, poor financial performance, and an inability to scale.

3. Ensure a Smooth Handover Process

Founders often possess deep institutional knowledge and an emotional connection to the company that can't be easily replaced. When professional CEOs are brought in, it's essential that they have the time and support needed to learn from the founder and establish trust with the leadership team and employees.

If the handover process is rushed or poorly managed, it can create confusion, insecurity, and a lack of alignment across the organisation. Employees may feel disconnected from the new leadership, and the CEO may struggle to gain the credibility needed to lead effectively. A smooth transition helps ensure that the company remains stable, and that the new CEO can build on the founder's legacy without alienating key stakeholders.

Eric Schmidt's transition to CEO of Google, briefly mentioned earlier, is a model of a well-executed handover process. Larry Page and Sergey Brin, the co-founders of Google, worked closely with Schmidt for years after bringing him on as CEO. Page and Brin remained actively involved in the company, serving as key advisors to Schmidt while focusing on product development and innovation. This collaborative approach allowed Google to maintain its innovative culture while benefiting from Schmidt's operational expertise.

In contrast, Uber, the ride-hailing giant founded by Travis Kalanick and Garrett Camp, had revolutionised the transportation industry, growing rapidly from its founding in 2009 to become a global powerhouse. However, Uber's meteoric rise was accompanied by a series of scandals, legal issues, and cultural problems, much of which stemmed from Kalanick's aggressive and confrontational leadership style. By 2017, Uber's toxic workplace culture and numerous regulatory challenges had reached a breaking point, and Kalanick was forced to resign under pressure from investors and the board.

After Kalanick's departure, Uber brought in Dara Khosrowshahi, the former CEO of Expedia, to stabilise the company and rebuild its reputation. Khosrowshahi was seen as a calm and measured leader, capable of steering Uber through its challenges and preparing the company for an eventual IPO. While Khosrowshahi made progress in addressing Uber's toxic culture and navigating regulatory issues, the transition was far from smooth, and Uber's IPO in 2019 was marked by disappointing financial performance and a significant drop in its valuation.

Kalanick had been both the company's greatest strength and its greatest weakness. The sudden departure of Kalanick created a leadership vacuum, and Uber struggled to maintain its aggressive growth strategy under new leadership. Khosrowshahi faced the difficult task of rebuilding trust with employees, regulators, investors, and riders, all while managing the operational complexities of a global business. Additionally, the cultural shift required to move away from Kalanick's combative style was challenging, as many employees had become accustomed to Uber's "win-at-all-costs" mentality.

Uber's experience underscores the importance of managing cultural change during a leadership transition. When a founder like Kalanick leaves under controversial circumstances, the incoming CEO must not only address the operational challenges but also work to repair the company's culture. A rushed or poorly managed transition can lead to long-lasting damage, both in terms of employee morale and public perception.

WeWork, the co-working space giant founded by Adam Neumann in 2010, became one of the most talked-about startups of the 2010s. Neumann's bold vision of transforming office space into a community-driven experience helped WeWork grow at an astonishing rate, attracting billions in investment and expanding to cities around the world. However, by 2019, Neumann's leadership style—marked by grandiosity, erratic behaviour, and questionable financial decisions—began to unravel, leading to one of the most dramatic collapses in recent business history.

After WeWork's failed IPO and mounting pressure from investors, Neumann was ousted as CEO in September 2019. WeWork appointed Artie Minson and Sebastian Gunningham as co-CEOs to lead the company through a period of restructuring. However, the damage to WeWork's reputation and finances was severe, and the company struggled to regain its footing. In 2020, Sandeep Mathrani, a seasoned real estate executive, was brought in as CEO to stabilise the business.

Neumann's unchecked leadership and excessive spending had left WeWork with massive losses, unrealistic growth targets, and a tarnished reputation. The company's reliance on Neumann's charismatic leadership made it difficult for the new CEOs to establish credibility with investors and employees. Moreover, the business model itself was fundamentally flawed, relying on rapid expansion without a clear path to profitability. The new leadership faced the immense challenge of turning around a company that had been built on hype and unsustainable growth.

Mathrani was himself replaced by David Tolley in 2023, who led the company through a tumultuous period of financial restructuring which ultimately ended with the company filing for Chapter 11 bankruptcy protection. Whilst writing this book WeWork emerged from bankruptcy after renegotiating 190 leases and exiting 170 locations—a far cry from the dizzy heights of an imminent IPO and a valuation of $47Billion. The company is now led by commercial real estate veteran John Santora.

WeWork's downfall illustrates the risks of over-reliance on a charismatic founder and the importance of financial discipline in scaling a business. When a founder's vision is too ambitious and detached from reality, the company can suffer long-term consequences. The transition to new leadership at WeWork was made more difficult by the need to fundamentally rethink the company's business model, which had been shaped entirely by Neumann's vision.

4. Leverage the Founder's Strengths in a Strategic Role

In many successful transitions, the founder doesn't disappear entirely but instead takes on a new strategic role within the company. This allows the company to benefit from the founder's unique vision and expertise while allowing the professional CEO to manage day-to-day operations. By positioning the founder as a chairman, board member, or advisor, companies can ensure continuity while avoiding the pitfalls of over-reliance on the founder's leadership.

Founders often bring unparalleled insight into the company's culture, customer base, and competitive landscape. Keeping the founder involved in a strategic capacity allows the company to leverage this knowledge while ensuring that the CEO has the autonomy needed to lead effectively. This approach can also help ease concerns from investors, employees, and customers who may worry about the company's direction after the founder steps down.

Nike's founder Phil Knight transitioned from CEO to chairman of the board, where he continued to play a key strategic role in the company's direction. Knight's ongoing involvement allowed Nike to maintain its innovative culture and strong brand identity while scaling under the leadership of professional CEOs. By remaining a guiding force in the company, Knight ensured that Nike stayed true to its founding principles even as it grew into a global leader in sportswear.

SECTION THREE

Principles of Founder Mode Leadership

Chapter 13
The Power of First Principles Thinking

First principles thinking is a problem-solving approach that involves breaking down complex problems into their most fundamental elements and building solutions from the ground up. This method enables founders to challenge conventional wisdom, question assumptions, and come up with innovative solutions to problems that others may deem unsolvable. By focusing on the core truths of a problem, founders can rethink industries and develop groundbreaking products and services.

In this chapter, we will explore how several founders, have applied first principles thinking to solve complex problems and reinvent their respective industries. These founders leveraged this approach to disrupt traditional business models and build companies that defy expectations.

First Principles Thinking: What It Is and Why It Matters

First principles thinking involves stripping away preconceived notions and assumptions to understand the most fundamental components of a problem. Once these elements are identified, innovative solutions can be crafted by reconstructing the problem from a base level.

This approach forces individuals to move beyond incremental improvements and rethink the entire structure of a problem or industry. In founder mode, this type of thinking is invaluable, as it enables leaders to challenge outdated business models, develop radical solutions, and overcome seemingly insurmountable obstacles.

Reinventing the Thermostat with First Principles

Tony Fadell, co-founder of Nest and a key figure behind the development of the iPod at Apple, is another founder who applied first principles thinking to revolutionise an everyday product: the home thermostat.

When Fadell and his team set out to create the Nest Learning Thermostat, they started by asking fundamental questions about why thermostats were so inefficient and difficult to use. Traditional thermostats required users to manually adjust the temperature, often leading to wasted energy. Fadell applied first principles thinking to break down the problem into its most basic elements: people want comfort in their homes, but they also want to save energy without having to constantly adjust their thermostat.

Fadell and his team developed a thermostat that could learn users' behaviour and preferences, automatically adjusting the temperature to save energy while maintaining comfort. By focusing on the fundamental problem of balancing comfort and energy efficiency, Fadell was able to create a product that disrupted the home automation market and paved the way for the rise of smart home devices.

Disrupting Payments with Stripe

Patrick Collison, co-founder of Stripe, applied first principles thinking to solve one of the biggest challenges for online businesses: accepting payments. Before Stripe, payment processing for online transactions was complicated, slow, and expensive, requiring businesses to navigate complex systems that were often inefficient.

Collison and his brother John Collison recognised that the core problem with online payments was the outdated infrastructure that businesses were forced to use. Instead of accepting the complexity of traditional payment gateways, the Collisons applied first principles thinking to develop a simpler, more flexible solution. They built Stripe from the ground up, creating a platform that allowed businesses to integrate payment processing seamlessly into their websites with just a few lines of code.

Stripe's approach revolutionised online payments, making it easier for businesses to accept payments and scale globally. By questioning the complexity of existing payment systems and focusing on the most fundamental needs of businesses, the Collisons built a company that has become a critical infrastructure for the internet economy.

Applying First Principles Thinking Across Industries

First principles thinking isn't limited to tech or consumer products—it can be applied across a wide range of industries to solve entrenched problems, overcome complex challenges, and drive significant innovation. By breaking problems down into their most basic elements and challenging the assumptions that underpin traditional business models, founders in industries like healthcare, transportation, and education have reinvented the way these sectors operate.

Healthcare: Elizabeth Holmes and the Promise—and Peril—of First Principles Thinking

Elizabeth Holmes, founder of Theranos, is one of the most infamous examples of how first principles thinking can be both promising and dangerous when misapplied. Holmes set out to revolutionise the healthcare industry by simplifying blood testing. She questioned why blood tests required large volumes of blood and why the process was so time-consuming and expensive. By applying first principles thinking, Holmes envisioned a device that could test for multiple diseases using just a single drop of blood. This innovation had the potential to dramatically lower costs, increase accessibility, and improve the patient experience.

While Holmes applied first principles thinking to question the fundamentals of blood testing, the technology behind her vision did not live up to the promises. Despite her bold claims and the billions raised in venture capital, Theranos' device failed to deliver accurate results, ultimately leading to the company's collapse and a high-profile trial. The case of Theranos underscores the importance of rigorous testing and validation, especially in industries like healthcare where the stakes are incredibly high.

Transportation: The Boring Company and Rethinking Urban Transportation

Elon Musk, through The Boring Company, has applied first principles thinking to reimagine how cities approach transportation infrastructure. Musk's idea for The Boring Company originated from his frustration with traffic congestion and the limitations of traditional road systems. Rather than accepting the high cost and inefficiency of building more roads or expanding public transportation systems, Musk applied first principles thinking to question why we should rely solely on surface-level transportation.

Musk proposed an underground network of tunnels where electric vehicles, or "pods," could travel at high speeds, bypassing surface-level congestion. By focusing on the core problem—inefficiency in urban transportation—Musk and his team developed a solution that eliminates many of the constraints of above-ground infrastructure, such as weather, space limitations, and high costs. The Boring Company's tunnels are designed to be smaller, faster to build, and less expensive than traditional underground railway or road construction projects.

While The Boring Company's full vision has yet to be realised on a large scale, the application of first principles thinking has allowed Musk to challenge conventional assumptions about how cities should solve their traffic problems and explore new, more efficient alternatives.

Education: Democratising Learning

Sal Khan, founder of Khan Academy, applied first principles thinking to rethink education and make high-quality learning accessible to everyone. Before founding Khan Academy, Khan identified several key issues with traditional education: it was expensive, limited to specific geographical locations, and often delivered in a one-size-fits-all format that didn't cater to individual learning speeds or styles.

Khan approached the problem by questioning the core components of education—what is needed for someone to learn effectively, and why is high-quality education restricted to certain people? He concluded that the rise of the internet offered a way to democratise education by providing free, high-quality learning materials to anyone with an internet connection. Khan Academy's video-based learning platform allowed students to learn at their own pace, in any location, and revisit concepts as needed.

By challenging the traditional model of classroom-based learning, Khan created a platform that has helped millions of students worldwide and changed the way educators think about personalised learning. The concept of flipped classrooms, where students learn material at home and do hands-on work in class, is one such innovation that has been influenced by Khan's approach.

Energy: Clean Energy Adoption

Lyndon and Peter Rive, co-founders of SolarCity, applied first principles thinking to tackle the complex challenge of clean energy adoption. The Rives, along with their cousin Elon Musk, questioned why the adoption of solar energy was so slow, despite its potential to reduce carbon emissions and lower energy costs. They recognised that one of the key barriers was the high upfront cost of installing solar panels, along with the complexity of navigating government incentives and energy regulations.

Simplifying the path to solar energy: Instead of focusing solely on improving solar panel technology, the Rives applied first principles thinking to the entire process of solar adoption. SolarCity introduced an innovative financing model that allowed homeowners to install solar panels with little or no upfront cost, paying for the energy produced by the panels over time. This made solar energy more accessible to a wider range of customers and removed one of the biggest financial barriers to clean energy adoption.

SolarCity's business model, combined with its focus on simplifying the customer experience, helped drive the adoption of residential solar power across the United States. While SolarCity was eventually acquired by Tesla, its approach to solving the core problem of cost and accessibility continues to influence the solar energy market.

Biotechnology: Jennifer Doudna and CRISPR

Jennifer Doudna, co-developer of the revolutionary CRISPR gene-editing technology, is a powerful example of how first principles thinking can lead to breakthroughs in biotechnology. Doudna and her team applied first principles thinking to the problem of genetic modification, asking how they could develop a tool that would allow scientists to precisely target and edit specific genes in living organisms.

CRISPR's development represented a significant departure from traditional methods of genetic engineering, which were often slow, expensive, and imprecise. By focusing on the fundamental mechanics of how bacteria defend themselves against viruses (a process known as CRISPR), Doudna and her collaborators were able to develop a tool that could be used to edit DNA with unprecedented precision.

CRISPR has since been hailed as one of the most significant discoveries in modern biology, with applications ranging from curing genetic diseases to improving crop yields. Doudna's work has opened the door to a wide range of possibilities in biotechnology, many of which were previously considered impossible or impractical.

Chapter 14
Iterative Experimentation in Founder Mode

In founder-led companies, one of the defining characteristics is a fast-paced, iterative approach to experimentation. Founders often rely on rapid cycles of testing, learning, and improving to drive innovation, make critical decisions, and achieve breakthrough results. This contrasts sharply with the more deliberate, data-driven approaches that are typical in traditional management, where larger organisations prioritise detailed analysis and methodical planning before implementing changes.

This chapter will explore how founders use iterative experimentation to push boundaries, react to market feedback, and scale their businesses quickly. We will also look at the benefits and challenges of this approach and how it contrasts with slower, more structured approaches in traditional management.

The Mindset of Iterative Experimentation

At the heart of iterative experimentation is a mindset that values learning through action. Founders often operate with the belief that quick, small experiments lead to faster insights than extended periods of planning and analysis. This mindset allows them to innovate in real time, pivot when necessary, and respond to customer feedback and market conditions with agility.

Founders typically work under conditions of uncertainty, with limited resources and rapidly changing environments. In these circumstances, speed is critical. Rather than waiting for perfect data or an exhaustive analysis, founders prioritise taking action, collecting feedback, and iterating based on real-world results. This approach allows them to move quickly and learn from failures without being paralysed by indecision.

Iterative experimentation also allows founders to remain flexible and adaptable. In the early stages of a company, the business model, product offering, and target market are often in flux. By embracing small, iterative experiments, founders can test different hypotheses, refine their product, and adjust their strategy without committing too many resources to any one direction.

The Speed vs. Accuracy Trade-Off

One of the fundamental differences between iterative experimentation in founder mode and traditional management approaches is the trade-off between speed and accuracy. In traditional management, companies often prioritise making data-driven decisions based on extensive research and analysis, seeking to minimise risk before implementing changes. While this approach reduces the likelihood of errors, it can also slow down the pace of innovation and make it difficult to respond to dynamic market conditions.

In contrast, founders tend to prioritise speed over accuracy, accepting that some decisions will lead to failure or suboptimal results. However, they view these failures as opportunities to learn and refine their approach quickly. This emphasis on speed allows founders to test more ideas in a shorter period, ultimately leading to better outcomes through trial and error.

Founders who embrace iterative experimentation understand the value of "failing fast." By quickly identifying what doesn't work, they can pivot to new ideas and refine their approach before too many resources are wasted. This process of rapid experimentation and course correction is crucial in the early stages of a startup when resources are limited, and the window for finding product-market fit is narrow.

Instagram, founded by Kevin Systrom and Mike Krieger, is a prime example of a company that used iterative experimentation to find success. Originally launched as a location-based social network called Burbn, the app had limited traction. Systrom and Krieger quickly realised that users were more interested in the photo-sharing feature of the app than its other functionalities. They stripped down the app to focus solely on photo-sharing, iterating quickly to launch Instagram in its current form. This rapid pivot, driven by iterative experimentation, allowed Instagram to capture the attention of millions of users and become one of the most successful social platforms in the world.

Building a Culture of Experimentation

For iterative experimentation to be effective, it must become part of the company's culture. In founder-led companies, this culture often begins with the founder's own approach to risk-taking and problem-solving. A culture of experimentation empowers employees to think creatively and act independently. When employees feel that they have the freedom to test new ideas without fear of failure, they are more likely to push the boundaries of what's possible and come up with innovative solutions. This culture also promotes collaboration and transparency, as teams openly share their results—both successes and failures—and learn from each other's experiments.

Contrasting with Traditional Management Approaches

Traditional managers often prefer to wait until they have sufficient data to support a decision, which can result in missed opportunities in dynamic industries. In contrast, founders in startup mode recognise that waiting for perfect data is a luxury they cannot afford. They move forward with experiments even when the data is incomplete, trusting that they can make adjustments along the way based on real-world results.

Both approaches have their merits, and the key is for founders to know when to prioritise speed and experimentation over analysis and precision. For fast-growing startups, particularly in the early stages, iterative experimentation is often the more effective approach, as it allows companies to move quickly and test different paths to success.

In traditional companies like Procter & Gamble (P&G), the approach to product development is typically driven by extensive research and long-term planning. P&G relies on detailed consumer insights, focus groups, and pilot programmes before launching new products. While this method ensures that products are thoroughly tested and optimised, it contrasts with the faster, more iterative approach favoured by many startup founders and can limit the number of products brought to market.

Rapid Product Development: Iterating on Features and User Experience

One of the most common uses of iterative experimentation is in product development, particularly in tech startups. Rather than waiting until a product is fully perfected before launching, founders often release a minimum viable product (MVP) and then iterate based on user feedback. Crucially, releasing an MVP rather than holding back a release until it has all the features listed on the roadmap enables the start-up to generate revenue earlier, and build a customer base who, in turn, become beta testers and solution advocates.

Dropbox, founded by Drew Houston and Arash Ferdowsi, is a textbook example of iterative experimentation in product development. In the early stages, Dropbox released a simple MVP that allowed users to easily store and sync files across devices. Instead of spending years developing a fully-featured product, Houston and his team focused on a core feature that solved a specific pain point—file sharing across devices. They then used customer feedback to guide the development of additional features, such as shared folders, team collaboration tools, and integrations with other platforms.

Dropbox's success can be attributed to its willingness to launch early and iterate quickly, continuously improving the user experience based on real-world feedback. The company avoided the trap of over-building (potentially in a direction the market wouldn't value) and instead honed in on what users actually wanted.

Pivoting Business Models Through Experimentation

Iterative experimentation isn't limited to product features; it's also a key strategy for refining business models. In the early stages of a startup, founders often experiment with different ways of monetising their products or services, testing various pricing models, distribution channels, and customer segments. By iterating on their business model, founders can find the most effective path to profitability without committing too many resources to a single approach.

Building Stronger Customer Relationships Through Iteration

Another critical area where iterative experimentation is applied is in building and refining customer relationships. Founders often experiment with different ways of engaging customers, understanding their needs, and responding to feedback. By iterating on their communication strategies, customer support processes, and user experiences, founders can create a more customer-centric business that fosters loyalty and long-term relationships.

Glossier, the beauty brand founded by Emily Weiss, is a strong example of how iterative experimentation can be used to build a customer-first brand. Weiss launched Glossier as a direct-to-consumer beauty brand after running a popular beauty blog called *Into The Gloss.* She used her blog's community to gather insights into what customers wanted from beauty products, allowing her to test different formulations, packaging, and marketing strategies before launching Glossier.

Weiss continued to iterate on Glossier's product offerings and customer experience by actively engaging with her customer base through social media, surveys, and focus groups. This ongoing dialogue allowed Glossier to rapidly respond to customer preferences, creating a product line that resonated with its core audience. The brand's success is a testament to the power of iterative experimentation in building strong, long-term relationships with customers.

Rapid Testing in Marketing and Growth Strategies

Marketing is another area where iterative experimentation plays a crucial role, especially for founder-led companies looking to scale quickly. Rather than committing to a single marketing strategy, founders often test different messaging, channels, and campaigns to see what resonates most with their target audience. This iterative approach allows them to quickly identify the most effective ways to acquire and retain customers without spending large amounts of time or money on strategies that may not work.

Navigating Product-Market Fit Through Iteration

Achieving product-market fit is one of the most critical milestones for any startup. Founders use iterative experimentation to test different product features, pricing models, and customer segments to find the right combination that meets market demand. This process often involves multiple iterations and adjustments based on customer feedback and real-world performance.

One of the most iconic pivots in tech history is the transformation of Odeo into Twitter. Originally a platform to help users discover and subscribe to podcasts, Odeo faced a critical moment when iTunes began to dominate the podcast space. Rather than give up, the founders took a bold approach, asking their team to generate new ideas. Jack Dorsey and Biz Stone's concept of a status-updating micro-blogging platform emerged, and with it, Twitter was born—a decision that forever changed the landscape of social media.

TransferWise, now Wise, began as a simple solution for low-cost international money transfers. Founders Taavet Hinrikus and Kristo Käärmann iterated based on early customer feedback, gradually adding new currencies, enhancing user experience, and introducing features like multi-currency accounts. By continuously refining their offering to meet customer needs and simplifying the process of sending money abroad, Wise was able to scale rapidly and find product-market fit, becoming a major disruptor in the financial services industry.

Chapter 15
Bias for Action: How Speed Drives Innovation

In the world of startups and founder-led companies, speed often takes precedence over perfection. Founders, working in fast-paced, competitive environments, understand that waiting for the perfect solution can mean missing out on crucial opportunities. Instead, they prioritise action, making quick decisions, launching products with minimal features, and iterating based on real-world feedback. This "bias for action" is one of the defining characteristics of successful founders and is a key driver of innovation and growth in fast-moving markets.

This chapter will explore why founders frequently choose speed over perfection, how rapid iteration fuels growth, and the impact of this mindset on long-term innovation. We'll examine examples of founders and companies that have embraced this bias for action and used it to their advantage.

Why Founders Prioritise Speed Over Perfection

A bias for action allows founders to test ideas, fail fast, and learn faster. By prioritising speed, they're able to stay ahead of competitors, capitalise on emerging trends, and adjust their strategies based on real-world insights rather than theoretical plans. By acting quickly and iterating based on feedback, they can adapt to market conditions and customer needs more effectively than if they waited for the "perfect" solution.

Etsy, founded by Rob Kalin in 2005, embraced speed over perfection from its inception. The e-commerce platform for handmade goods started as a small-scale project designed to help artists and crafters sell their products online. Instead of waiting to develop a fully-featured marketplace, Kalin and his team quickly built a basic platform and launched it to test the concept. As the platform grew, Etsy iterated rapidly, adding new features and improving user experience based on feedback from both sellers and buyers. Today, Etsy is a global marketplace with millions of active users, thanks to its early bias for action.

Canva, the online design platform co-founded by Melanie Perkins, applied rapid iteration as a key strategy for growth. When Canva first launched, it offered a basic tool for non-designers to create simple graphics. Perkins and her team prioritised speed, launching the platform with only the most essential features. As users provided feedback, Canva rapidly iterated, adding new design tools, templates, and integrations that responded directly to customer requests. This continuous improvement process allowed Canva to expand its user base and become one of the leading design platforms globally.

Canva's ability to launch quickly and improve continuously has been instrumental in its success. Rather than waiting for a fully-fledged product, Perkins focused on getting the platform into the hands of users and using their feedback to guide future development.

Overcoming Analysis Paralysis

One of the greatest advantages of a bias for action is that it helps founders avoid analysis paralysis, a situation where excessive planning and overthinking prevent progress.

Houzz, the home design platform co-founded by Adi Tatarko and Alon Cohen, grew rapidly by embracing a bias for action and avoiding analysis paralysis. Tatarko and Cohen started Houzz as a side project after struggling to find home design inspiration for their own renovation. Instead of spending years researching the market, they quickly built a simple website that allowed users to browse and save design ideas. As more users joined the platform, the founders iterated rapidly, adding new features like a marketplace for home products and professional services.

By taking action and learning from early users, Houzz grew into a leading platform for home design and renovation, with millions of users and a thriving community. The founders' bias for action allowed them to capitalise on the growing demand for online design resources and expand the platform quickly.

Driving Long-Term Innovation Through Rapid Iteration

In many industries, the companies that win are those that innovate the fastest. This approach ensures that innovation is not a one-time event but an ongoing process that fuels growth over time.

Squarespace, founded by Anthony Casalena, used rapid iteration to fuel long-term innovation in the website-building space. When Casalena launched Squarespace, it started as a simple platform for building websites with minimal coding knowledge. However, as the company grew, Casalena and his team continuously iterated on the platform, adding new design templates, e-commerce capabilities, and integrations with third-party tools. By prioritising speed and iteration, Squarespace has remained a leading player in the highly competitive no-code website-building market, constantly introducing new features to meet the evolving needs of its users.

Casalena's bias for action has been instrumental in Squarespace's success, allowing the company to compete with the likes of Wix and WordPress by rapidly improving its product offering.

Chapter 16
Building a Visionary Product Roadmap

One of the most important responsibilities for founders is creating a product roadmap that aligns with their long-term vision while remaining flexible enough to adapt to market changes and evolving customer needs. A product roadmap serves as a strategic guide that outlines the direction of a company's product development efforts over time, providing clarity on key milestones, features, and goals. However, in founder mode, building a visionary roadmap involves more than just a linear path—it requires balancing ambition with adaptability.

In this chapter, we will explore how founders craft visionary product roadmaps that serve as blueprints for innovation, growth, and market leadership. We'll also look at examples of founders who have successfully used their roadmaps to guide their companies through different stages of development, while remaining responsive to changes in the market.

Defining the Long-Term Vision

The foundation of any successful product roadmap is the long-term vision. This vision should reflect what the founder wants the company to achieve over the next several years, not just in terms of product features, but in how the company will make an impact on its customers, its industry, and the world at large. A visionary roadmap is one that goes beyond incremental improvements, pushing the boundaries of what's possible and setting ambitious goals for the future—A North Star, if you will.

Founders often possess a unique ability to see beyond the immediate needs of the market and anticipate future trends. This forward-thinking perspective allows them to create roadmaps that position their companies as industry leaders, capable of shaping the direction of the market.

Zoom, founded by Eric Yuan, provides a compelling example of how a clear long-term vision can drive product development. From the beginning, Yuan's vision for Zoom was to create a video conferencing platform that was simple, reliable, and scalable, with the potential to transform communication across businesses and industries. Despite entering a crowded market with established players like Skype and WebEx, Zoom's long-term vision focused on creating a superior user experience with minimal friction, prioritising ease of use and high-quality video and audio.

Yuan's roadmap for Zoom emphasised constant improvements in performance, reliability, and scalability, all while maintaining the core simplicity that set the platform apart. This long-term focus allowed Zoom to rapidly scale and become a critical tool for businesses, educational institutions, and individuals during the COVID-19 pandemic, cementing its position as a leader in the video conferencing space.

A visionary product roadmap begins with a clear, long-term vision that serves as the guiding light for all product development decisions. This vision should push the company to innovate and differentiate itself from competitors while addressing the current needs of customers and anticipating future trends.

Prioritising Features That Drive Impact

Another critical aspect of building a visionary product roadmap is prioritising features that will have the most significant impact on the company's growth and customer satisfaction. Founders are often faced with numerous ideas and feature requests (the feature backlog), but it's essential to focus on the elements that align with the company's vision and provide the most value to users.

Effective product roadmaps don't try to do everything at once. Instead, they prioritise the features and improvements that will move the needle in terms of user adoption, customer retention, revenue, and market differentiation. Founders must weigh the potential impact of each feature against the resources required to develop and launch it, ensuring that the roadmap remains focused on the most critical objectives.

Calendly, founded by Tope Awotona, is a scheduling tool that simplifies the process of setting up meetings. Awotona's vision for Calendly was to create a seamless, user-friendly platform that eliminated the back-and-forth of scheduling via email. Rather than trying to build a broad set of features from the start, Awotona focused the product roadmap on perfecting the core scheduling functionality and creating integrations with popular calendar tools like Google Calendar and Outlook.

As Calendly gained traction, Awotona and his team carefully prioritised features that enhanced the scheduling experience, such as group scheduling, custom availability settings, and workflow automation. By focusing on the most impactful features, Calendly grew rapidly and became a go-to tool for professionals and businesses looking to streamline their scheduling processes.

Founders must prioritise the features that will have the greatest impact on their product's success. By focusing on high-impact features that align with the company's vision, founders can drive growth, stay front of mind, stay relevant, and ensure that their roadmap remains focused on delivering value to customers.

Setting Realistic Milestones and Timelines

While it's important for founders to think big and be ambitious, it's equally important to set realistic milestones and timelines in their product roadmaps. A roadmap that is too ambitious can lead to missed deadlines, frustrated teams, and disappointed customers. Conversely, a roadmap with clear, achievable milestones helps keep the company on track and ensures steady progress toward the long-term vision.

Duolingo, the language-learning platform co-founded by Luis von Ahn, demonstrates the importance of setting realistic milestones in a product roadmap. Von Ahn's long-term vision for Duolingo was to make language learning accessible to everyone, regardless of their financial resources. To achieve this, Duolingo launched as a free platform with a gamified learning experience, focusing on delivering high-quality language lessons that were both effective and fun.

As the platform grew, Duolingo's roadmap included ambitious goals, such as expanding the number of languages offered and incorporating advanced learning features like speech recognition and personalised practice sessions. However, von Ahn and his team broke these goals down into manageable milestones, ensuring that each new feature was carefully developed and tested before being released to users. This approach allowed Duolingo to grow steadily and maintain its reputation for delivering an engaging learning experience.

Navigating Challenges and Adjustments in the Product Roadmap

Creating a visionary product roadmap is not without its challenges. No matter how well-planned a product roadmap may be, founders will inevitably encounter unforeseen obstacles that require adjustments. These challenges can come in many forms—technical difficulties, resource constraints, changes in market demand, or external disruptions. A key part of building a visionary roadmap is the ability to respond to these obstacles without losing sight of the company's long-term goals.

Patreon, co-founded by Jack Conte, offers a great example of how founders can adapt their product roadmap in response to unexpected challenges. Patreon, a platform that allows creators to earn recurring revenue from their fans, initially focused on providing a simple way for artists to collect monthly payments. However, as the platform grew, Conte and his team encountered unexpected obstacles related to payment processing and creator retention.

To overcome these challenges, Patreon adjusted its roadmap to prioritise features that would help creators manage their businesses more effectively, such as analytics tools and membership management. By pivoting to address these pain points, Patreon not only retained its user base but also attracted more creators who saw the platform as essential for building sustainable careers. This ability to navigate obstacles without losing sight of the bigger picture allowed Patreon to evolve into a platform that better served its community.

Flexibility is essential for navigating unexpected obstacles in a product roadmap. Founders must be willing to make adjustments while keeping the long-term vision in focus, ensuring that their roadmap remains aligned with both internal and external realities.

One of the defining characteristics of a successful product roadmap is its ability to evolve in response to customer and market feedback. Founders who embrace this adaptability are able to refine their products, enhance their offerings, and seize new opportunities as they arise. By incorporating feedback into the roadmap, founders ensure that their products continue to meet customer needs while staying aligned with broader market trends.

Founders can create feedback loops that allow them to gather insights from customers, identify emerging trends, and assess the effectiveness of their product strategy. By continuously listening to customers and adapting the roadmap based on real-world usage and feedback, founders can stay ahead of the curve and avoid building features or products that don't resonate with their audience.

Figma, founded by Dylan Field, is an example of how a company successfully adjusted its product roadmap based on market feedback. Initially launched as a cloud-based design tool aimed at solo designers, Figma quickly realised that its real value lay in collaboration. After receiving feedback from early users, Field and his team shifted their focus toward building collaboration features that allowed design teams to work together in real-time. This pivot not only aligned Figma with the needs of design teams but also positioned the company as a leader in the growing field of collaborative design software.

By integrating customer feedback into its product roadmap, Figma was able to expand its user base, differentiate itself from competitors like Adobe, and create a product that became essential for design teams across industries.

Prioritising features and initiatives requires a clear understanding of what will drive the most value for the business and its customers. Founders must be willing to say no to certain features or projects, even if they are appealing, in order to stay focused on the most critical objectives. This ability to make tough trade-offs is key to ensuring that the roadmap remains manageable and that the company doesn't spread itself too thin.

Trello, co-founded by Michael Pryor and Joel Spolsky, faced prioritisation challenges as the company grew. Trello, a visual project management tool, quickly gained popularity due to its simplicity and flexibility. However, as the user base expanded, Pryor and his team were inundated with feature requests from customers who wanted more customisation options, integrations, and advanced functionality.

To keep the product roadmap focused and manageable, Pryor and his team had to make tough decisions about which features to prioritise. Rather than adding every requested feature, Trello focused on enhancing the core user experience and building integrations that would have the most significant impact on productivity. This disciplined approach to prioritisation allowed Trello to remain simple and user-friendly, while still addressing the needs of its growing customer base.

Effective communication is critical to the success of any product roadmap. As the company scales and the roadmap evolves, founders must ensure that all team members are aligned with the vision and understand how their work contributes to the broader goals of the company. Clear communication helps keep teams focused, motivated, and on track, even when adjustments need to be made to the roadmap.

Founders should communicate the rationale behind roadmap decisions, ensuring that teams understand why certain features are being prioritised and how they fit into the larger vision. Regular updates and open discussions about the roadmap can help prevent confusion and ensure that everyone is working toward the same goals.

Buffer, the social media management platform co-founded by Joel Gascoigne, has long prioritised transparency and communication in its product roadmap. Buffer's roadmap is publicly available, allowing both employees and customers to see what the company is working on and what features are in the pipeline. This open approach to communication has helped Buffer maintain alignment within the company while also fostering trust and engagement with its user base.

By clearly communicating the product roadmap and involving the team in discussions about prioritisation, Gascoigne has been able to keep Buffer's team focused and aligned, even as the company has grown and evolved. This transparency ensures that everyone understands the company's direction and how their work contributes to its success.

Chapter 17
Founder-Led Marketing: A Direct Connection to the Brand

In many founder-led companies, the marketing strategy is deeply intertwined with the founder's personal vision, story, and values. By being actively involved in the company's marketing, founders are able to shape a more authentic connection with their customers, often becoming the face of the brand and driving powerful narratives that resonate on a deeper level. This direct connection allows founders to communicate their vision, engage with customers, and build brand loyalty in ways that traditional corporate marketing teams may struggle to achieve.

In this chapter, we will explore how founder-led marketing creates a more authentic, relatable brand identity, and we'll examine examples of founders who have successfully positioned themselves as the face of their brands. We'll also discuss the benefits and challenges of this approach and how it contributes to long-term brand loyalty and growth.

The Power of Authenticity in Founder-Led Marketing

One of the most significant advantages of founder-led marketing is the authenticity it brings to the brand. Customers today crave authenticity—they want to support brands that align with their values and have a genuine story to tell. When founders take a hands-on approach to marketing, they can directly share their personal journey, vision, and passion, which creates a powerful emotional connection with the audience.

In an era of highly polished corporate messaging, consumers are often sceptical of brands that feel impersonal or purely profit-driven. Founder-led marketing, by contrast, offers a more personal touch. Founders can speak candidly about their struggles, successes, and motivations, which helps humanise the brand and build trust with customers. This level of authenticity is difficult to replicate in large organisations where marketing is often handled by teams of professionals who may not have the same emotional connection to the brand.

Glossier, founded by Emily Weiss, is a prime example of a founder-led brand that has successfully used authenticity as a core marketing strategy. Weiss, who started as a beauty blogger with her site *Into The Gloss*, built Glossier based on her deep understanding of beauty consumers and her passion for skincare and makeup. From the outset, Weiss was the face of Glossier, frequently engaging with customers on social media, sharing her personal beauty routine, and inviting feedback from her audience.

By positioning herself as a relatable and approachable figure, Weiss created a community-driven brand where customers felt like they were part of the product development process. Glossier's marketing was built on real conversations with consumers, and Weiss's authenticity and personal connection to the brand were instrumental in its rapid growth and loyal following.

Founders as the Face of the Brand

The personal connection between the founder and the brand can be a key differentiator in crowded markets, helping the company stand out and create a unique identity. When founders are willing to put themselves front and centre in marketing campaigns, interviews, and public appearances, they add a layer of credibility and relatability that can be highly effective in building brand loyalty.

Customers are more likely to trust a brand when they can see the person behind it. People, after all, buy from people. Moreover, when founders are the face of the brand, they can respond to challenges or crises more effectively by directly addressing customers in a transparent and authentic way.

Sara Blakely, founder of Spanx, is a standout example of a founder who successfully became the face of her brand. From the very beginning, Blakely was heavily involved in Spanx's marketing efforts, often appearing in advertisements, interviews, and promotional videos. Her personal story of bootstrapping Spanx with just $5,000, her determination to bring her product to market, and her humorous, down-to-earth personality resonated with millions of women.

Blakely's visibility as the face of Spanx helped the brand grow into a household name. Her hands-on approach to marketing, including her willingness to appear in product demonstrations and personally explain the benefits of Spanx products, gave the brand an authentic and relatable identity. Today, Spanx is a leader in the shapewear industry, in large part due to Blakely's personal connection with the brand and its customers.

Building Community Through Founder Engagement

Founders who actively engage with their customers through social media, events, and other platforms can create a loyal and engaged customer base that feels personally connected to the brand. This sense of community is especially valuable in today's consumer landscape, where customers increasingly seek brands that align with their personal values and offer more than just a transactional relationship.

Founder-led marketing often goes beyond traditional advertising and focuses on creating genuine connections with customers. By fostering a sense of community, founders can turn their customers into advocates who spread the word about the brand and help it grow organically. This community-driven approach not only strengthens brand loyalty but also provides valuable feedback that founders can use to improve their products and services.

Outdoor Voices, the activewear brand founded by Tyler Haney, built its marketing strategy around community engagement, with Haney playing an active role in connecting with customers. Haney's vision for Outdoor Voices was to promote "Doing Things"—an inclusive approach to fitness that encouraged people to get active in ways that felt fun and approachable. To build this community, Haney regularly hosted events, such as group workouts and outdoor activities, where she personally engaged with customers and promoted the brand's values.

The Challenges of Founder-Led Marketing

While founder-led marketing offers many advantages, it also comes with its own set of challenges. As companies grow, founders may find it difficult to maintain the same level of involvement in marketing while also managing other aspects of the business. Additionally, when the founder becomes the face of the brand, the company's reputation can become closely tied to the founder's actions, making it vulnerable if the founder faces public scrutiny or makes missteps.

As a company scales, founders need to find ways to maintain the authenticity and personal connection that initially drove the brand's success, while also delegating responsibilities to marketing teams. This balance can be difficult to achieve, as it requires founders to trust their teams to uphold the brand's values and voice, even as they step back from day-to-day marketing activities.

TOMS, founded by Blake Mycoskie, illustrates both the benefits and challenges of founder-led marketing. Mycoskie's personal story of founding TOMS based on the "One for One" giving model—where the company donates a pair of shoes to a child in need for every pair sold—became a central part of the brand's identity. Mycoskie's direct involvement in marketing, including public speaking, interviews, and charity events, helped TOMS grow into a widely recognised brand with a strong social mission.

However, as TOMS grew, it became more difficult for Mycoskie to maintain the same level of personal involvement in the company's marketing. Eventually, TOMS faced criticism for not fully living up to its social mission, and Mycoskie stepped down as CEO. This example highlights the challenges of scaling a brand that is so closely tied to the founder's personal story and values.

Scaling Founder Involvement in Marketing

Ben & Jerry's, co-founded by Ben Cohen and Jerry Greenfield, offers an example of how founders can scale their involvement in marketing while maintaining the brand's authenticity. In the early days of Ben & Jerry's, Cohen and Greenfield were heavily involved in promoting their ice cream brand, often appearing in company ads, public events, and media interviews to share their story and social mission. As the company grew, Cohen and Greenfield gradually reduced their day-to-day involvement in marketing but remained influential in shaping the brand's messaging and public image.

By hiring marketing professionals who understood and shared their vision, Ben & Jerry's was able to maintain its unique, socially conscious voice even as it expanded into a global brand. Cohen and Greenfield continued to play a role as brand ambassadors, participating in major campaigns and using their platform to advocate for social justice, while the company's marketing team handled the execution of day-to-day marketing activities.

Transitioning from Founder-Led to Team-Led Marketing

Founders must invest time in hiring and training marketing professionals who not only have the technical skills to execute marketing campaigns but also have a deep understanding of the brand's story, mission, and values. Founders should remain involved in setting the strategic direction for marketing, while empowering their team, and giving them the autonomy, to take ownership of the day-to-day execution.

Sweetgreen, the fast-casual salad chain co-founded by Nicolas Jammet, Jonathan Neman, and Nathaniel Ru, successfully transitioned from founder-led marketing to a team-led approach while maintaining its brand's authenticity. In its early days, the founders were highly visible in promoting Sweetgreen's mission of sustainable, locally sourced food, often appearing at events and in the media to share their story. As Sweetgreen expanded, the founders built a marketing team that was aligned with their vision and could carry the brand forward without their constant involvement.

Sweetgreen's marketing team continued to emphasise the brand's core values—sustainability, health, and community—while executing innovative campaigns that resonated with its target audience.

Maintaining a Personal Connection with Customers

Digital platforms provide founders with an opportunity to maintain a direct connection with their customers, even as the company grows. By sharing insights, updates, and behind-the-scenes content, founders can continue to engage with their audience in a way that feels personal and authentic, even if most of the marketing 'heavy lifting' is now executed by a dedicated team.

Bulletproof, the wellness brand founded by Dave Asprey, is a good example of how founders can maintain a personal connection with customers through digital platforms. Asprey, who is known for popularising Bulletproof Coffee and the biohacking movement, has built a strong personal brand around his wellness philosophy. He regularly shares insights through his blog, podcast, and social media channels, providing valuable content to his audience while promoting Bulletproof's products.

Even as Bulletproof has grown into a successful brand with a dedicated marketing team, Asprey remains actively involved in engaging with customers and promoting his vision for optimal health and performance. His personal connection with the brand has been a key driver of customer loyalty and has helped Bulletproof maintain its authenticity in a competitive wellness market.

Navigating the Risks of Founder-Led Marketing

While founder-led marketing offers many benefits, it also comes with risks. When a brand's identity is closely tied to its founder, the company's reputation can be vulnerable to any missteps or controversies involving the founder. As a result, founders need to be mindful of how their personal actions and statements reflect on the brand, particularly in today's highly scrutinised media environment.

Papa John's, founded by John Schnatter, is an example of how a founder's personal actions can negatively impact a brand's reputation. Schnatter was heavily involved in Papa John's marketing for years, often appearing in commercials and serving as the face of the brand. However, after Schnatter made controversial statements that sparked public backlash, the company faced significant reputational damage. Papa John's eventually distanced itself from Schnatter and rebranded to repair its image, highlighting the risks of closely associating a brand with its founder.

In the UK, those old enough to remember, will recall Gerald Ratner who inherited Ratners from his father. In just six years he had turned a small local business into one of the largest jewellery retailers in the world. However, within months of delivering a speech, in which he described one of his products as "crap," Ratners was reputationally and financially destroyed.

Founder-led marketing can expose a brand to risks if the founder's personal actions or statements damage the company's reputation. Founders must be mindful of how their behaviour reflects on the brand and take steps to mitigate risks, particularly as the company grows and becomes more visible.

Chapter 18
Leveraging Storytelling to Inspire and Lead

In founder mode, storytelling is one of the most powerful tools that leaders can use to inspire their teams, communicate their vision, and align the organisation around common goals. Storytelling goes beyond sharing facts and figures—it taps into the emotions, values, and motivations that drive people to take action. By crafting compelling narratives, founders can convey their mission, overcome challenges, and lead their teams with purpose and clarity.

This chapter will explore how founders use storytelling as a leadership tool, offering detailed insights into the techniques that successful founders employ to inspire their teams and communicate their long-term vision. We'll examine examples of founders who have built powerful brands and strong organisational cultures by harnessing the power of storytelling.

The Role of Storytelling in Leadership

Storytelling in leadership is about more than just sharing a company's history or product features—it's about creating a shared sense of purpose and helping people understand how their work contributes to something greater. Founders who are effective storytellers are able to articulate the "why" behind their company's mission, motivating their teams to work toward a common goal. This sense of shared purpose is essential for building strong, cohesive teams that are energised by the company's vision.

In fast-growing startups, there is often a sense of urgency and chaos. Teams are frequently asked to work long hours, adapt to new challenges, and pivot quickly in response to market conditions. In these environments, storytelling can be a powerful way to keep employees engaged and aligned, even when the path forward is unclear. Founders who use storytelling to explain the company's mission and core values help their teams stay focused on the bigger picture, fostering a sense of belonging and shared responsibility.

Ingvar Kamprad, the founder of IKEA, used storytelling to shape IKEA's culture and global success. Kamprad often shared the story of his humble beginnings in rural Sweden, where he started selling matches as a young boy, eventually growing into a furniture empire. This narrative of frugality, simplicity, and accessibility became central to IKEA's mission of 'democratic design'—furnishing homes with affordable, functional products. Kamprad's personal story inspired employees and customers alike, creating a sense of connection with IKEA's values of sustainability and innovation.

Using Storytelling to Communicate Vision

In founder mode, the vision is often ambitious and transformative, and it requires the support of the entire organisation to bring it to life. Storytelling allows founders to paint a picture of the future that is both aspirational and achievable, helping teams understand not only what they're working toward but why it matters.

When founders use storytelling to communicate their vision, they aren't just talking about the next quarter or the next product launch—they're sharing a long-term roadmap for the company's growth and impact. By framing the company's journey as an evolving narrative, founders can help their teams see how their contributions today will lead to larger successes down the road.

Ellevest, the financial platform founded by Sallie Krawcheck, provides a great example of how storytelling can be used to communicate a long-term vision. Krawcheck's vision for Ellevest was to create a financial platform that specifically served the needs of women, addressing the gender gap in financial literacy and investment opportunities. In sharing the story behind Ellevest, Krawcheck emphasised her own experiences as a woman in the male-dominated finance industry and her realisation that traditional financial services were not designed with women's unique goals and challenges in mind.

Krawcheck's storytelling helped to galvanise her team around the mission of empowering women to take control of their financial futures. By framing Ellevest's journey as part of a larger movement for gender equality, Krawcheck was able to inspire both her team and her customers, creating a brand that was not just about financial products but about driving meaningful social change.

Overcoming Challenges Through Storytelling

Founders frequently face obstacles and setbacks as they build their companies, and storytelling can be a powerful tool for overcoming these challenges. By sharing stories of past struggles and triumphs, founders can demonstrate resilience and perseverance, motivating their teams to push through difficult times. These stories help employees see that challenges are a natural part of the journey, and that the company's leadership is committed to finding solutions.

When founders are transparent about the challenges they've faced—whether it's a failed product launch, a funding shortfall, or a tough market environment—they create an atmosphere of openness and trust. Employees are more likely to stay engaged and committed when they know that their leaders have faced adversity and emerged stronger. Storytelling allows founders to contextualise challenges as part of the company's broader narrative, helping teams stay motivated and focused on the path ahead.

Rent the Runway, founded by Jennifer Hyman and Jennifer Fleiss, faced significant challenges in its early days as the company sought to disrupt the fashion rental market. Hyman often shares the story of how Rent the Runway struggled to convince high-end fashion designers to rent their garments to customers, as the concept was initially seen as risky and unproven. Hyman and Fleiss had to navigate numerous rejections and setbacks before finally securing partnerships with key designers, which helped validate their business model.

By sharing these stories of rejection and perseverance, Hyman built a culture of resilience within Rent the Runway. Her transparency about the challenges the company faced helped to foster a sense of determination and grit among the team, encouraging employees to stay focused on the company's long-term vision even when facing obstacles. This storytelling also reinforced the idea that innovation often requires persistence in the face of adversity. This powerful form of storytelling ultimately helped prepare the company for its IPO in 2021.

Building a Strong Organisational Culture Through Storytelling

Founders have the unique ability to shape their company's culture through the stories they tell. Whether it's a story about how the company grew from humble beginnings or a tale of how a customer's life was changed by the product, these narratives serve as cultural touchstones that guide employee behaviour and decision-making. Founders who are intentional about storytelling can use it to build a culture that reflects their values and supports the company's long-term success.

Tom's of Maine, co-founded by Tom Chappell, built its organisational culture around stories of environmental sustainability and social responsibility. From the beginning, Chappell emphasised that Tom's of Maine was not just a company that made natural personal care products—it was a company that cared deeply about its impact on the planet and its communities. Chappell's storytelling helped to create a culture where employees were motivated by more than just profit—they were driven by a sense of purpose and a commitment to ethical business practices.

By regularly sharing stories of the company's environmental initiatives, charitable donations, and community partnerships, Chappell reinforced the values that were central to Tom's of Maine's culture. This storytelling helped to attract employees who were aligned with the company's mission and created a sense of pride and ownership among the team.

Techniques for Effective Storytelling in Leadership

Becoming an effective storyteller is a critical skill for founders who want to inspire their teams, communicate their vision, and build trust both within and outside the organisation. Storytelling in leadership isn't just about telling anecdotes—it's about crafting compelling narratives that resonate with the audience, whether that's employees, customers, investors, or partners.

Crafting a Compelling Narrative

At the heart of effective storytelling is the ability to craft a narrative that resonates with the audience on both an intellectual and emotional level. Founders need to structure their stories in a way that captures attention, creates engagement, and leaves a lasting impact. A compelling narrative often includes three key elements: a challenge or problem, a journey or struggle, and a resolution that aligns with the company's mission and values.

Many successful stories follow the structure of the hero's journey—think *Star Wars*—a narrative arc that includes the world before, (the pain point the founder's company seeks to solve) a protagonist, (in this case, the founder, the product, or the company), an obstacle or challenge, (the market, legacy competitors etc.) and the ultimate triumph, (mass adoption of the founder's product and all is right with the world). This structure works because it taps into universal human experiences of overcoming adversity and achieving success. By positioning the company's story within this framework, founders can create a narrative that inspires and motivates their teams.

BrewDog, the Scottish craft beer company founded by James Watt and Martin Dickie, built its brand on a rebellious, anti-establishment narrative. Frustrated with the bland, mass-produced beers dominating the market, the founders set out to create bold, flavourful brews that challenged the status quo. BrewDog's story of sticking it to 'big beer' resonated with consumers who wanted something different and authentic. By crafting a narrative around independence, innovation, and community, BrewDog inspired a loyal following and transformed the craft beer industry.

Using Storytelling to Build Trust

Stories that feel genuine and authentic are far more likely to build trust than those that come across as overly polished or insincere. By being open and transparent in their storytelling, founders can create an environment of honesty and even vulnerability that fosters deeper connections with their audience.

Away, the travel brand co-founded by Jen Rubio and Steph Korey, used storytelling to build trust with its customers and investors from the very beginning. Rubio's personal story of struggling with broken luggage on a trip and her frustration with existing luggage options was the catalyst for founding Away. This narrative of solving a real-world problem resonated deeply with customers, as it highlighted Away's commitment to designing high-quality, durable luggage that addressed common travel pain points.

Throughout the company's growth, Rubio and Korey continued to use storytelling to build trust with their audience, whether by sharing behind-the-scenes insights into product development or acknowledging challenges the company faced. This authenticity helped Away cultivate a loyal customer base and build strong relationships with investors, who were drawn to the founders' transparency and dedication to solving real problems.

When and Where to Use Storytelling

The impact of storytelling is often amplified when it is delivered at the right time and in the right context. Founders should be strategic about when and where they use storytelling to inspire their teams or communicate with external stakeholders. The best stories are those that are relevant to the current situation, whether it's during a period of rapid growth, a challenging market environment, or a major product launch.

Founders can use storytelling during key moments of transition or change, such as when introducing a new strategic direction, launching a new product, or rallying the team during difficult times. In these moments, storytelling can help to create a sense of momentum, unity, and clarity, helping teams understand the "why" behind the company's actions and decisions.

KIND Snacks, founded by Daniel Lubetzky, has used storytelling at key moments in the company's growth to communicate its mission of making healthier, more transparent snack options available to consumers. Lubetzky frequently shares the story of how his father, a Holocaust survivor, inspired him to build a company that was rooted in kindness and doing the right thing. This narrative has been woven into KIND's marketing and internal messaging, particularly during pivotal moments such as product expansions and partnerships. This helped to align both the team and the customers with KIND's mission, reinforcing the company's long-term vision.

Chapter 19
Adaptability in the Face of Market Shifts

One of the defining characteristics of successful founders is their ability to adapt in the face of market shifts. While having a clear vision and strategy is essential, market conditions can change rapidly, requiring founders to pivot, adjust, and reinvent their approach. Founders who possess flexibility and resilience are able to navigate these changes, capitalise on new opportunities, and keep their companies on a growth trajectory. Adaptability is often the difference between a company that stagnates and one that thrives.

In this chapter, we will explore the critical role adaptability plays in founder-led companies, examining how founders pivot in response to market changes and why resilience is a key attribute in uncertain environments.

The Importance of Adaptability in Founder-Led Companies

Markets are rarely static, and successful companies are those that can evolve alongside changing circumstances. Founders need to cultivate a mindset that embraces change rather than fears it. This involves being open to new ideas, continuously learning, and being willing to challenge assumptions about their business model, products, and customers. Founders who demonstrate adaptability can pivot quickly when market conditions shift, ensuring that their companies remain competitive and positioned for long-term success.

Warby Parker, co-founded by Neil Blumenthal and Dave Gilboa, is a great example of a company that has demonstrated adaptability in the face of market changes. Originally launched as an e-commerce platform for affordable prescription glasses, contact lenses, and sunglasses, Warby Parker recognised early on that there was growing demand for an omnichannel experience. Rather than sticking solely to its online model, Warby Parker adapted by opening physical retail locations, allowing customers to try on glasses in person while still offering the convenience of online ordering.

This pivot allowed Warby Parker to tap into a broader customer base, blending the best of both digital and in-store experiences. The company's ability to adapt to shifting consumer preferences helped it scale rapidly and become a major player in the eyewear market. Warby Parker's success demonstrates the importance of being flexible and responsive to market trends, even when it means evolving beyond the company's original business model.

When and How to Change Course

One of the most challenging aspects of pivoting is knowing when it's the right time to make a change. Founders must be able to assess whether the obstacles they're facing are temporary or indicative of a deeper problem with their business strategy. A successful pivot often comes from a willingness to listen to customer feedback, analyse market trends, and recognise when the initial vision needs to be refined or adapted.

Slack, founded by Stewart Butterfield, is a well-known example of a successful pivot. Slack was originally developed as an internal communication tool for Butterfield's team while they were working on a video game called Glitch. When it became clear that the game wasn't gaining traction, Butterfield and his team decided to pivot away from gaming and focus on the communication tool they had built. That tool became Slack, which quickly became a dominant player in the workplace communication and collaboration space.

Butterfield's willingness to pivot from the original vision of building a game to developing a completely different product—one that solved a pressing need for many organisations—demonstrated the importance of flexibility and resilience in the face of market shifts. Slack's success as a communication platform underscores how a well-timed pivot can lead to substantial growth.

Resilience: The Mindset That Drives Adaptability

Every founder faces setbacks at some point—whether it's a failed product launch, a funding shortfall, or an unexpected competitor entering the market. What sets resilient founders apart is their ability to maintain their determination and optimism, using these setbacks as learning experiences rather than reasons to give up. Resilient founders are more likely to take calculated risks, experiment with new approaches, and recover from failure more quickly.

Pandora, the music streaming platform founded by Tim Westergren, is a prime example of resilience in action. In the early 2000s, Pandora struggled to find a viable business model as it faced mounting financial difficulties and the collapse of the dot-com bubble. Westergren and his team worked for years without pay, believing in the potential of their platform to revolutionise music discovery. Despite numerous challenges, including a failed attempt to raise venture capital, Westergren refused to give up.

Eventually, Pandora pivoted from a subscription-based service to an ad-supported model, which allowed it to grow rapidly and become one of the leading music streaming platforms. Westergren's resilience and willingness to keep adapting the business model in response to market feedback were key to Pandora's time in the spotlight.

The Role of Data and Market Feedback in Adaptability

One of the key factors that enable founders to adapt effectively is their ability to gather and act on data and market feedback and constantly challenge the sunk cost fallacy. Successful founders don't rely on intuition alone—they use data to make informed decisions about when to pivot, which markets to target, and how to refine their product offering. By staying close to their customers and listening to them, founders can identify emerging opportunities and adjust their strategy before it's too late.

Data-driven decision-making is critical for ensuring that pivots and strategic shifts are based on solid insights rather than guesswork. Founders who actively seek out customer feedback, monitor key performance indicators, and stay attuned to broader market trends are better equipped to adapt to changes in their industry. This approach allows founders to make more informed decisions about where to focus their efforts and resources.

Zappos, founded by Nick Swinmurn and later led by Tony Hsieh, is a great example of a company that used data and customer feedback to adapt and grow. Zappos started as an online shoe retailer, but Hsieh quickly realised that the key to success in e-commerce, particularly when size really matters, was providing exceptional customer service. Zappos adapted its business model to prioritise customer satisfaction, offering free shipping, a 365-day return policy, and 24/7 customer support.

By listening to customer feedback and analysing what was driving repeat business, Zappos was able to differentiate itself from competitors and build a loyal customer base. The company's focus on customer service became its defining characteristic, helping it grow into one of the most successful online retailers and eventually leading to its acquisition by Amazon.

Gusto, a payroll and HR software company founded by Joshua Reeves, developed a culture of flexibility that allowed it to pivot and adapt as the market evolved. Originally focused on simplifying payroll for small businesses, Gusto recognised that many of its customers needed more than just payroll services—they needed a full suite of HR tools to manage benefits, compliance, and employee engagement. By fostering a culture of flexibility, Gusto expanded its offerings to include HR, benefits, and insurance services, becoming an all-in-one platform for small business owners.

Reeves encouraged a culture where teams were empowered to explore new opportunities and experiment with different product features. This flexibility allowed Gusto to pivot quickly in response to customer needs and expand its market reach, ultimately becoming a leading player in the HR software space.

Encouraging Experimentation and Risk-Taking

Founders who promote experimentation allow their teams to explore new ideas, even if those ideas don't always succeed. By learning from both successes and failures, companies can adapt more quickly and refine their strategies based on real-world data.

Buffer, the social media management platform co-founded by Joel Gascoigne, is an example of a company that embraced experimentation as a core part of its strategy. Buffer initially launched as a simple tool to schedule social media posts, but over time, Gascoigne and his team experimented with new features and business models to better serve their customers. For instance, Buffer experimented with a freemium model, offering free and paid plans to test which approach would drive the most growth.

This willingness to experiment allowed Buffer to adapt to changes in the social media landscape, continuously improving its product and staying relevant in a highly competitive market. Buffer's iterative approach helped the company refine its offerings and attract a loyal customer base.

The Role of Leadership in Adaptability

ClassPass, the fitness subscription platform founded by Payal Kadakia, offers a strong example of leadership in adaptability. When Kadakia first launched ClassPass, it started as a search engine for fitness classes. However, the initial model didn't gain traction, and

Kadakia quickly realised that she needed to pivot. Instead of sticking to the original idea, Kadakia and her team developed a new business model that allowed users to pay a subscription fee for unlimited access to fitness classes at various studios.

Throughout this pivot, Kadakia remained transparent with her team, communicating the reasons for the change and involving them in the process. Her leadership and resilience helped ClassPass navigate the pivot successfully, and the company eventually became a leader in the fitness subscription industry. Kadakia's ability to lead by example, embracing flexibility and involving her team in the adaptation process, was critical to ClassPass's success.

Founders must lead by example when it comes to adaptability. By being transparent, resilient, and open to change, founders can inspire their teams to embrace flexibility and stay focused on the company's long-term goals.

That being said, while adaptability is crucial for navigating market shifts, it's important for founders to balance flexibility with staying true to their long-term vision. Pivoting too frequently or losing sight of the company's core mission can lead to confusion and lack of focus. Founders who are overly reactive to every market change risk diluting their company's vision and confusing employees and the market they are seeking to serve. It's essential to differentiate between temporary trends and significant market shifts that require a strategic response.

Chapter 20
Managing Crises in Founder Mode

Founders are no strangers to crises. Whether it's financial trouble, product failures, regulatory challenges, or market disruptions, founders often find themselves in high-pressure situations that require swift decision-making and resilience. What sets founders apart from traditional corporate leaders is their ability to manage crises in unconventional ways. Instead of relying solely on standard protocols or hierarchical decision-making, founders often draw on their deep emotional investment in their company, creativity, and close-knit team dynamics to navigate uncertainty.

In this chapter, we will explore how founders manage crises differently than professional managers, with a focus on the unique methods they employ to steer their companies through turbulent times. We'll study examples of founders who successfully overcame crises by thinking outside the box, taking bold actions, and leveraging their direct connection to the company's mission and team.

The Founder's Emotional Investment in Crisis Management

One of the defining characteristics of founder-led crisis management is the intense emotional investment founders have in their companies. Founders aren't just managing an asset—they've often built their company from the ground up, and they view its success or failure as deeply personal. This emotional connection can drive founders to go above and beyond during a crisis, pushing them to find creative solutions and take risks that a professional manager might avoid.

A founder's personal connection to their company can lead to a heightened sense of responsibility and commitment during a crisis. This often means that founders are more willing to take bold actions, make difficult decisions, and mobilise their teams effectively with a sense of urgency. Emotional investment can also help founders maintain their focus and resilience in the face of adversity, as they feel personally accountable for the company's survival.

Cashing in on Brand Equity

In a crisis, the ability to make rapid decisions is crucial, as delays can exacerbate problems or lead to missed opportunities. Founders tend to bypass the layers of bureaucracy that can slow down decision-making in traditional corporate structures, allowing them to act quickly and mobilise their teams more effectively.

In times of crisis, a founder's personal brand equity and inherent connection to the company's mission can be valuable assets. Founders who have built strong personal brands are often able to rally external support, whether it's from investors, customers, or the media. By leveraging their personal credibility and the company's mission, founders can build trust and confidence in their ability to lead the company through difficult times.

The Long-Term Impact of Crisis Management in Founder Mode

The way founders manage crises can have a profound long-term impact on their companies. While crises often present immediate challenges, they also serve as pivotal moments that shape the future direction of the business, foster resilience, and influence organisational culture. Founders who navigate crises successfully often emerge stronger, with a more unified team, a refined business strategy, and a deeper understanding of the company's strengths and weaknesses.

Founders who use crises as opportunities to innovate demonstrate to their teams that adaptability is a core strength of the organisation. By encouraging employees to think creatively and embrace change during difficult times, founders can build a culture where innovation becomes a regular part of the company's DNA. This culture of adaptability allows the company to remain agile, responsive, and competitive in a fast-changing market.

JetBlue, founded by David Neeleman, faced a major crisis in 2007 when a snowstorm grounded planes and left passengers stranded on the tarmac for hours, causing widespread public outrage. The incident, which became known as the "Valentine's Day Massacre," severely damaged JetBlue's reputation and led to significant operational challenges. However, Neeleman's response to the crisis was pivotal in turning the situation around.

Rather than downplaying the issue, Neeleman took full responsibility and used the crisis as an opportunity to improve JetBlue's operations. The company introduced a Customer Bill of Rights, which outlined compensation for delays and cancellations, and implemented new procedures to prevent similar incidents in the future. JetBlue also invested in technology to improve communication and flight management during weather disruptions. These innovations not only helped JetBlue recover from the crisis but also positioned the airline as a customer-centric leader in the industry.

Crises often force founders to reevaluate their business strategies and make necessary adjustments to survive and thrive in a new reality. Whether it's shifting market conditions, financial pressures, or regulatory changes, crises can reveal underlying weaknesses in a company's business model or highlight new opportunities for growth. Founders who use crises as a time for strategic reflection can emerge with a more focused and effective business plan.

Nasty Gal, the fashion e-commerce brand founded by Sophia Amoruso, experienced rapid growth in its early years but faced significant financial difficulties and operational challenges as the company expanded. By 2016, Nasty Gal filed for bankruptcy after struggling to maintain profitability and manage its growing workforce. However, instead of letting the company's financial collapse define its legacy, Amoruso used the crisis as an opportunity to refine her vision and pursue new ventures.

After Nasty Gal was sold to Boohoo Group, Amoruso launched Girlboss, a media platform focused on empowering women in business. Through Girlboss, Amoruso leveraged her experiences—both her successes and her failures—with Nasty Gal to inspire and educate a new generation of female entrepreneurs. The crisis that initially seemed like a major setback for Amoruso ultimately led to the development of a more focused and impactful business strategy with Girlboss.

Lush, the cosmetics company co-founded by Mark Constantine, faced a major crisis in 2007 when one of its suppliers was found to be using palm oil, which contributed to deforestation and environmental damage. This revelation threatened Lush's reputation as an ethical and environmentally conscious brand. Instead of downplaying the issue, Constantine took swift action, publicly acknowledging the problem and committing to eliminating palm oil from Lush's products.

Lush's transparency and commitment to environmental responsibility turned the crisis into a defining moment for the brand. The company's decision to reformulate its products without palm oil rein-forced its values and strengthened its relationship with customers who were passionate about sustainability. Lush's response to the crisis not only preserved the company's reputation but also enhanced its standing as a leader in ethical business practices.

Chapter 21
Founder Mode Beyond Startups: Lessons for Big Companies

The principles of founder mode are often associated with fast-moving startups that thrive on innovation, rapid decision-making, and a deep connection to the company's mission. However, as companies scale, they can lose the agility and boldness that defined their early days. Larger organisations face more bureaucracy, risk aversion, and slower decision-making processes, which can stifle innovation. Yet, many of the principles that define founder mode—adaptability, a customer-first mentality, and a relentless drive for innovation—can be applied in larger organisations to help them remain agile and competitive in fast-evolving markets.

In this chapter, we will explore how larger organisations can adopt and integrate founder mode principles to retain the entrepreneurial spirit that drives innovation. We'll look at examples of companies that have successfully applied these principles long after scaling and discuss how leaders in big organisations can embrace a founder-led mindset to remain relevant in an increasingly competitive landscape.

Retaining Agility Through Decentralised Decision-Making

One of the defining characteristics of founder mode is the ability to make quick, autonomous decisions. In startups, founders often bypass bureaucracy and make fast decisions, allowing them to respond to market opportunities and challenges with agility. As companies scale, decision-making processes typically become more centralised, which can slow down innovation. However, larger organisations that want to remain agile can adopt decentralised decision-making, empowering teams to act autonomously while still aligning with the company's overall vision.

Decentralising decision-making allows teams within a larger organisation to operate with the same level of autonomy as a small startup. By granting individual teams or business units the freedom to experiment, innovate, and make decisions quickly, companies can maintain their ability to respond rapidly to market changes. This approach reduces bottlenecks and encourages a culture of experimentation and risk-taking.

Haier, the Chinese multinational home appliances and consumer electronics company, is an example of a large organisation that has successfully applied founder mode principles through decentralised decision-making. Under the leadership of Zhang Ruimin, Haier transformed its organisational structure into a network of small, autonomous business units called "micro-enterprises." These micro-enterprises operate with significant autonomy, allowing them to quickly respond to customer needs and market demands.

By adopting this decentralised approach, Haier has maintained its ability to innovate despite its size. Each micro-enterprise operates almost like a startup within the larger organisation, with the freedom to develop new products, test ideas, and make decisions without waiting for approval from senior leadership. This structure has enabled Haier to remain competitive in the fast-paced electronics and appliances market, continually introducing new products and adapting to changing consumer preferences.

Maintaining a Customer-First Mentality

Founder-led companies are often deeply connected to their customers, with founders personally invested in understanding customer needs and delivering value. As companies grow, this close connection to the customer can weaken, leading to a more transactional relationship. Larger organisations that want to retain the innovative spirit of founder mode must prioritise maintaining a customer-first mentality, ensuring that customer feedback and needs remain central to decision-making processes.

LEGO, the Danish toy company, provides a strong example of how a large organisation can maintain a customer-first mentality even after scaling. In the early 2000s, LEGO faced a financial crisis as its product lines became overly complex and disconnected from customer preferences. The company made a bold decision to simplify its offerings and focus on core products that resonated with its customers. LEGO also began actively engaging with its fan community, involving customers in product development through initiatives like LEGO Ideas, a platform that allows fans to submit their own designs for potential production.

By maintaining a close connection to its customers and prioritising their feedback, LEGO was able to refocus its business and rebuild its brand. The company's customer-first mentality helped it re-establish itself as a leader in the toy industry, driven by products that were closely aligned with customer interests and needs.

Fostering a Culture of Innovation and Risk-Taking

Innovation and risk-taking are central to founder mode, but as companies grow, risk aversion can creep in. Larger organisations often develop processes and structures that prioritise stability over innovation, which can slow down the development of new ideas. To retain the innovation-driven culture that defines founder mode, big companies must foster an environment where experimentation and risk-taking are encouraged and rewarded.

Creating a safe space for innovation: In founder-led companies, the willingness to take risks and experiment is often key to developing breakthrough products and services. Larger organisations can adopt this mindset by creating "innovation labs" or dedicated teams or departments that focus on exploring new ideas, testing new technologies, and developing products outside the constraints of the core business. These spaces allow employees to take risks, fail, learn, and iterate in a safe environment without the fear of failure impacting the broader organisation.

3M, the multinational conglomerate known for products like Post-it Notes and Sellotape, has long fostered a culture of innovation through its "15% rule." This rule allows employees to spend 15% of their work time pursuing projects or ideas outside of their normal job responsibilities. This freedom to explore and experiment has led to some of 3M's most iconic products, including the invention of the Post-it Note, which came about through a failed adhesive experiment.

By encouraging risk-taking and innovation through dedicated programmes, 3M has managed to maintain the entrepreneurial spirit of founder mode even as the company has grown into a global giant. This culture of experimentation continues to drive product development and keeps 3M at the forefront of innovation in multiple industries.

Google (now part of Alphabet) has famously adopted a "startup within a company" approach through its Google X division, often referred to as the company's "moonshot factory." Google X operates independently of Google's core business and focuses on developing breakthrough technologies that could reshape entire industries, such as self-driving cars, smart contact lenses, and high-altitude internet balloons. The autonomous structure of Google X allows its teams to experiment freely, without the constraints of Google's traditional business model or short-term revenue expectations.

By fostering this type of autonomous innovation, Alphabet is able to maintain its reputation as a cutting-edge tech company, even as it has grown into a massive global conglomerate. The "startup within a company" model has allowed Google X to take risks and innovate in ways that would be difficult within the structure of a more traditional large company.

Preserving the Founder's Vision and Values

As companies grow, it can be challenging to maintain the founder's original vision and values, especially when leadership transitions occur, or new layers of management are added. However, preserving the founder's core vision and values is essential for maintaining a strong company culture and ensuring that the company's mission remains intact. Larger organisations can apply founder mode principles by keeping the founder's vision central to their operations and decision-making processes, even after the company has scaled.

IKEA, founded by Ingvar Kamprad, has managed to preserve the founder's vision and values even as it has grown into one of the world's largest home furnishing companies. Kamprad's original vision was to create affordable, well-designed furniture for everyday people, and this mission has remained at the heart of IKEA's business model. Despite its global scale, IKEA has maintained a commitment to cost-consciousness, sustainability, and simplicity—core values that Kamprad instilled in the company.

IKEA's leadership has worked hard to ensure that the founder's vision continues to guide the company's strategy and culture, even as it expands into new markets and faces increasing competition. By staying true to Kamprad's original mission, IKEA has maintained its unique identity and customer loyalty while scaling globally.

Building Cross-Functional Teams

Cross-functional teams can recreate the dynamism of a startup by fostering collaboration, speeding up decision-making, and promoting innovative solutions to complex problems. These teams can be tasked with specific projects or initiatives, allowing them to move quickly and make decisions without waiting for approval from multiple layers of management.

Unilever, one of the world's largest consumer goods companies, has embraced cross-functional teams as part of its commitment to innovation and sustainability. Unilever's Sustainable Living Plan, which aims to reduce the company's environmental footprint while increasing its positive social impact, is driven by cross-functional collaboration. Teams from marketing, product development, sustainability, and supply chain management work together to create products that align with Unilever's sustainability goals.

Emphasising a Customer-Centric Culture

In founder-led startups, customer feedback is often at the heart of decision-making. Larger organisations can replicate this approach by creating formal processes for gathering and acting on customer insights. This might involve setting up customer advisory boards, conducting regular surveys, or engaging directly with customers through social media and other platforms.

Hilton Worldwide, the global hospitality company, has embraced a customer-centric approach through its Hilton Honors loyalty programme and its focus on personalised customer experiences. Hilton uses customer feedback to continually refine and improve its offerings, ensuring that it meets the evolving needs of travellers. For example, Hilton introduced the Connected Room feature, which allows guests to control room settings like temperature, lighting, and TV channels through their smartphones. This innovation was driven by feedback from customers who wanted more personalised and convenient hotel experiences.

Hilton's emphasis on customer-centricity extends to its employees, who are trained to prioritise guest satisfaction and address customer needs quickly and effectively. By putting the customer at the centre of its business, Hilton has maintained a strong reputation for service excellence while remaining competitive in the hospitality industry.

SECTION FOUR

Pitfalls, Challenges, and Evolving as a Founder

Chapter 22
Founder Burnout: Recognising and Preventing It

Building a company from the ground up is one of the most demanding and rewarding experiences for founders. However, the intense pressure to succeed, relentless work hours, and emotional investment in the business often put founders at high risk of burnout. Founder mode, with its fast-paced decision-making, high expectations, and personal accountability, can make it difficult for founders to step back, prioritise self-care, and maintain a healthy work-life balance. Ignoring the risks of burnout can have devastating consequences—not only for the founder's health but also for the business they've worked so hard to build.

In this chapter, we will explore the risks of burnout and mental health challenges that founders face while in founder mode. We will discuss the warning signs of burnout, how it can impact both personal well-being and business performance, and provide actionable strategies for founders to balance their intensity with self-care. By recognising and addressing burnout early, founders can create sustainable habits that support both their health and the long-term success of their companies.

Understanding Founder Burnout

Burnout is a state of emotional, mental, and physical exhaustion caused by prolonged stress and overwork. For founders, burnout often stems from the high stakes involved in building and running a company. The constant pressure to meet targets, secure funding, manage a growing team, and navigate crises can lead to overwhelming levels of stress. When combined with the personal sacrifices founders often make—such as long work hours, minimal sleep, and neglecting personal relationships—the risk of burnout increases significantly.

Founders often feel a deep sense of responsibility for their company's success, making it difficult for them to delegate tasks or step away from work. Many founders operate with an "always-on" mindset, believing that the more hours they put in, the more successful their company will be. This intense level of commitment can make it difficult to recognise when stress levels have become unsustainable, leading to burnout before the founder realises they're at risk.

Caterina Fake, co-founder of Flickr, experienced burnout while building the photo-sharing platform. In an interview, Fake described how the constant pressure to grow Flickr and meet the expectations of users, investors, and her team eventually took a toll on her health and well-being. After Flickr was acquired by Yahoo, Fake decided to take a step back from the company to prioritise her mental health and recover from the burnout she had experienced. Her decision to step away was a turning point, allowing her to regain her energy and later return to entrepreneurship with a renewed focus on balance and self-care.

Warning Signs of Burnout

Burnout doesn't happen overnight—it builds up over time. Founders who are aware of the warning signs can take action before burnout reaches a critical stage. Recognising these early indicators allows founders to implement changes that can prevent burnout from worsening.

Common warning signs of burnout:

- **Physical and mental exhaustion**: Constant fatigue, difficulty sleeping, and feeling drained even after resting are key signs of burnout. Founders may find it harder to focus or make decisions as their energy levels drop.
- **Cynicism and detachment**: Founders experiencing burnout often become emotionally detached from their work. What once brought excitement and fulfilment may start to feel burdensome or unimportant. Cynicism about the business, the market, or the team may increase.
- **Decreased productivity and motivation**: Burnout can lead to a decline in productivity, creativity, and problem-solving ability. Founders may struggle to complete tasks, experience brain fog, or feel unmotivated to tackle new challenges.
- **Neglecting personal relationships and self-care**: Founders experiencing burnout may start to withdraw from personal relationships and neglect their physical and mental well-being. This can include skipping meals, avoiding exercise, and ignoring personal hobbies or interests.

Arianna Huffington, co-founder of The Huffington Post, experienced a significant health scare caused by burnout. In 2007, after years of working long hours and neglecting her health, Huffington collapsed from exhaustion and broke her cheekbone. This wake-up call prompted her to reevaluate her relationship with work and led her to become a vocal advocate for workplace wellness and self-care.

Huffington's experience highlighted how even the most successful founders can experience burnout if they don't prioritise their health.

The Impact of Burnout on Business Performance

Burnout not only affects founders on a personal level but can also have serious consequences for the business. When a founder is burned out, their ability to lead, make decisions, and drive the company forward is significantly compromised.

Founders set the tone for the company's culture and direction. When a founder is burned out, it can create a ripple effect throughout the organisation. Employees may notice a lack of energy or focus from the founder, leading to decreased morale and productivity across the team. In severe cases, burnout can result in the founder stepping down or making critical mistakes that harm the company's growth trajectory.

Rand Fishkin, founder of Moz, experienced burnout after years of leading the SEO software company through rapid growth. Fishkin has spoken openly about how the stress of managing Moz, coupled with the pressure to deliver results to investors, led to severe burnout and depression. His burnout eventually led him to step down as CEO in 2014. In hindsight, Fishkin recognised that his decision-making had been impaired by burnout and that his mental health struggles had affected the company's performance during a critical time of expansion. Since then, Fishkin has become an advocate for mental health awareness among entrepreneurs.

Strategies for Preventing Burnout and Balancing Self-Care

Preventing burnout requires intentional effort and the development of healthy habits that support both mental and physical well-being. Founders who prioritise self-care and establish boundaries are better equipped to manage stress and maintain the energy needed to lead their companies.

Practical strategies for preventing burnout:

- **Set boundaries and delegate**: One of the most effective ways to prevent burnout is for founders to set clear boundaries between work and personal life. This may involve delegating tasks to trusted team members, learning to say no to non-essential meetings, or establishing specific work hours to avoid overworking.
- **Prioritise sleep, nutrition, and exercise**: Founders should make their physical health a priority by ensuring they get adequate sleep, eat nutritious meals, and incorporate regular exercise into their routines. These habits help to maintain energy levels and improve mental clarity.
- **Schedule time for hobbies and relaxation**: Taking time away from work to pursue hobbies, spend time with family and friends, or engage in relaxation activities is essential for maintaining mental balance. Founders should schedule time for activities that bring joy and relaxation.
- **Practice mindfulness and stress management**: Incorporating mindfulness practices such as meditation, yoga, or journaling can help founders manage stress and stay grounded during challenging times.

David Heinemeier Hansson, co-founder of Basecamp, is known for his advocacy of a healthy work-life balance. Hansson has long emphasised the importance of working reasonable hours, taking vacations, and maintaining a calm, focused approach to running a business. At Basecamp, Hansson and his co-founder, Jason Fried, have implemented a 40-hour workweek policy and encourage employees to prioritise their personal lives. This philosophy has helped Basecamp avoid the burnout culture that often plagues tech startups and has contributed to the company's long-term sustainability.

Building a Sustainable Founder Mindset

Building a sustainable mindset is key for founders who want to maintain their well-being and continue leading their companies effectively over the long term. In the face of constant pressures, high expectations, and demanding workloads, developing the right mindset can help founders manage stress, avoid burnout, and cultivate resilience.

Cultivating Resilience and Mental Toughness

While all founders face setbacks, obstacles, and stress, resilient founders are better able to recover from challenges and continue pushing forward. Developing resilience involves building mental toughness, embracing failure as part of the journey, and maintaining a long-term perspective that helps founders navigate short-term setbacks.

Founders with a growth mindset believe that their abilities can be developed through dedication and hard work, rather than being fixed traits. This mindset helps founders view challenges as opportunities for learning rather than as failures. Embracing a growth mindset allows founders to maintain their motivation and persistence, even when faced with difficult circumstances.

Ben Chestnut, co-founder of Mailchimp, exemplifies resilience in the face of adversity. When Chestnut and his co-founder started Mailchimp, they initially offered web design services. However, after struggling to gain traction in that market, they pivoted to focus on email marketing, which ultimately became the core of their business. Mailchimp's growth was gradual, with Chestnut often reflecting on the patience and persistence required to build the company. By embracing failure and adapting to market feedback, Chestnut was able to turn Mailchimp into a successful, bootstrapped business. His resilience helped him navigate the ups and downs of entrepreneurship without burning out.

Managing Stress Through Mindfulness and Reflection

Mindfulness practices such as meditation, deep breathing exercises, and journaling can help founders stay present, manage their emotions, and avoid being overwhelmed by stress. These practices help reduce anxiety, improve concentration, and foster a sense of calm, even in the midst of demanding work environments. Regular reflection also allows founders to step back, assess their priorities, and make more thoughtful decisions.

Evan Williams, co-founder of Twitter and Medium, has been a longtime advocate of mindfulness and meditation as tools for managing the stress of entrepreneurship. Williams has spoken openly about how meditation helps him stay centred and focused during times of high pressure. His mindfulness practice allows him to maintain a sense of balance and perspective, even when managing the complexities of running high-profile tech companies. Williams credits mindfulness with helping him make better decisions and avoid burnout.

Establishing Boundaries and Work-Life Balance

One of the biggest challenges for founders is setting boundaries between work and personal life. The "always-on" culture of entrepreneurship can make it difficult to disconnect from work, leading to constant stress and eventual burnout. Founders must establish clear boundaries and prioritise work-life balance in order to maintain their energy and well-being over the long term.

Founders who set boundaries are able to create space for rest, relaxation, and personal fulfilment outside of work. This might mean limiting work hours, scheduling regular breaks, or designating specific times for family, hobbies, and self-care. By enforcing these boundaries, founders can recharge their mental and physical energy, leading to greater productivity and creativity when they are at work.

Stewart Butterfield, co-founder of Slack, is known for his commitment to maintaining a healthy work-life balance. Butterfield encourages his team at Slack to work reasonable hours and avoid the long, gruelling schedules that are often associated with startup culture. He emphasises the importance of disconnecting from work and taking time off to recharge. Butterfield himself follows this philosophy, ensuring that he takes breaks and spends time with his family, even while managing the growth of a high-profile tech company.

Creating a Support System

No founder should face the challenges of entrepreneurship alone. Having a strong support system—whether it's a mentor, coach, co-founders, or a personal network—can make a significant difference in preventing burnout. A support system provides emotional encouragement, advice, and accountability, helping founders navigate difficult moments and stay on track with their personal and professional goals.

Mentors and peers who have been through the entrepreneurial journey can offer valuable perspective and guidance. They can help founders navigate challenges, make better decisions, and avoid common pitfalls that can lead to burnout. Founders should also cultivate relationships with individuals outside of their work environment, such as family members or friends, who can offer support and help them maintain a sense of balance.

Tristan Walker, founder of Walker & Company Brands, has spoken about the importance of having mentors and a strong support network throughout his entrepreneurial journey. Walker credits his mentors with helping him navigate difficult business decisions and avoid burnout by offering perspective and advice. In addition to his mentors, Walker has emphasised the value of surrounding himself with a supportive team and community, which has helped him stay grounded and maintain his energy as a founder.

Delegating and Trusting the Team

Effective delegation not only reduces the risk of burnout but also empowers the team to take ownership and contribute to the company's success.

Delegating tasks allows founders to focus on the areas where they can add the most value, rather than getting bogged down in day-to-day operational details. By trusting their team to handle key responsibilities, founders can free up time for strategic thinking, rest, and personal development. This balance leads to better decision-making and long-term sustainability for both the founder and the company.

Emily Weiss, founder of Glossier, is known for building a strong leadership team that she trusts to handle various aspects of the company's operations. As Glossier grew, Weiss recognised the importance of delegation and empowered her team to take ownership of product development, marketing, and customer experience. By trusting her team, Weiss was able to focus on high-level strategy and vision, preventing burnout while ensuring that Glossier continued to innovate and grow.

Chapter 23
Founder Blind Spots: Overcoming the Echo Chamber

Founders often possess a strong sense of vision and conviction that drives their company forward. However, this focus can sometimes lead to blind spots, where founders become insulated from alternative viewpoints or critical feedback. This "echo chamber" effect occurs when founders surround themselves with individuals who share their opinions and reinforce their ideas, rather than challenging their assumptions or offering dissenting perspectives. While confidence in a vision is important, failing to acknowledge blind spots can lead to poor decision-making, missed opportunities, and even organisational stagnation.

In this chapter, we will explore common blind spots that founders face and discuss the risks of operating within an echo chamber. We will examine the importance of fostering dissenting opinions and encouraging diverse perspectives within the team to counter these blind spots. By welcoming alternative viewpoints, founders can make more informed decisions, foster innovation, and build a stronger, more resilient organisation.

Understanding Founder Blind Spots

Blind spots occur when founders overlook critical factors that could impact their company's success. These blind spots are often a result of cognitive biases—such as confirmation bias, overconfidence, or groupthink—that lead founders to prioritise their own perspectives and discount opposing views. Founders may also become overly focused on certain aspects of the business, such as product development or scaling, while neglecting other areas that need attention.

Operating with blind spots can have serious consequences for both the founder and the company. Without diverse perspectives, founders may miss warning signs of market shifts, overlook customer feedback, or fail to anticipate competitive threats. Blind spots can also lead to a lack of innovation, as founders may be unwilling to question their own assumptions, adapt to new trends, or embrace fresh perspectives from their team or the market.

Elizabeth Holmes, founder of Theranos, serves as a well-known example of how founder blind spots can lead to disastrous outcomes. Holmes was deeply convinced of her vision to revolutionise the healthcare industry with a breakthrough blood-testing device. However, she operated within an echo chamber, surrounding herself with individuals who supported her narrative while ignoring dissenting voices—both within the company and from external critics. Despite mounting evidence that the technology was flawed, Holmes and her team continued to push forward, ultimately leading to the company's collapse and legal consequences.

The Theranos case highlights the dangers of blind spots and the importance of fostering a culture where dissenting opinions and critical feedback are encouraged. Had Holmes been more open to alternative perspectives and internal scepticism, the company's downfall *might* have been avoided.

The Risks of an Echo Chamber

An echo chamber is created when founders limit the diversity of perspectives in their decision-making process. In this environment, dissenting voices are silenced, and the founder's ideas are reinforced by those around them. While it may be comforting to receive constant validation, an echo chamber can lead to groupthink, where critical thinking and creativity are suppressed in favour of consensus.

Echo chambers often form because founders naturally gravitate toward individuals who share their values, ideas, and goals. Additionally, team members may be hesitant to challenge the founder's authority, especially in a fast-paced startup environment where the founder's vision is seen as the driving force behind the company's success. This dynamic can lead to a lack of constructive debate and a reluctance to raise concerns or offer alternative viewpoints.

When founders operate within an echo chamber, they are less likely to consider new approaches or challenge assumptions that may no longer be relevant. This can result in poor decision-making, missed opportunities for innovation, and an inability to adapt to changing market conditions. The absence of dissenting opinions can also lead to a culture of complacency, where employees are discouraged from speaking up or offering ideas that challenge the status quo.

HubSpot, a leading inbound marketing and sales platform, experienced a period of groupthink that CEO Brian Halligan later acknowledged. As HubSpot rapidly grew, the company became heavily focused on its core marketing platform and scaling the business. However, internal blind spots emerged as the leadership team became insulated from diverse perspectives. This led to slower innovation and a failure to anticipate customer needs in areas outside of marketing, such as sales enablement and customer service.

Recognising this, Halligan made a concerted effort to break out of the echo chamber by encouraging more open debate and fostering diverse perspectives within the team. He introduced a culture of "disagree and commit," where employees were encouraged to voice their disagreements during discussions but align behind the final decision once it was made. This shift in culture helped HubSpot regain its innovative edge and expand its product offerings.

Fostering Dissent and Diverse Perspectives

To avoid blind spots and break free from the echo chamber, founders must create an environment where team members feel comfortable challenging the status quo and offering alternative viewpoints without fear of retribution. By encouraging healthy debate, founders can uncover potential risks, explore new ideas, and make more informed decisions.

Building a team with diverse backgrounds, experiences, and perspectives is one of the most effective ways to counter blind spots. Diversity of thought leads to more robust discussions and prevents the team from falling into the trap of groupthink. Founders should prioritise hiring individuals from different industries, cultures, and disciplines to ensure that the team brings a wide range of ideas and solutions to the table.

Ed Catmull, co-founder of Pixar Animation Studios, is known for fostering a culture of candid feedback and constructive dissent. At Pixar, Catmull implemented a process called "The Braintrust," where filmmakers present their work to a group of peers who offer direct, honest feedback. The Braintrust sessions are designed to challenge ideas, identify weaknesses, and encourage filmmakers to think critically about their work. Importantly, the feedback is given in a spirit of collaboration, with the goal of making the final product stronger. This culture of open debate has been a key factor in Pixar's consistent delivery of high-quality, innovative films.

Katherine Power, co-founder of Who What Wear and Versed Skincare, has built her companies with a strong emphasis on diversity and inclusion. Power has actively sought out team members from diverse backgrounds, including those with different perspectives on fashion, beauty, and consumer preferences. By prioritising diversity,

Power has been able to develop products and brands that resonate with a wide range of customers and stay ahead of industry trends.

Mentors who have experience in the founder's industry or have navigated similar challenges can help founders see the bigger picture and avoid common pitfalls. Advisors can also introduce founders to new ideas, trends, or strategies that they may not have considered. Founders should actively seek out mentors or advisors who bring diverse perspectives and are willing to challenge their thinking.

Zalando, the European fashion e-commerce giant founded by Robert Gentz and David Schneider, implemented an internal feedback system called the "Radical Agility" framework. As part of this framework, Zalando's leadership team holds regular feedback sessions where employees at all levels are encouraged to share their opinions and challenge leadership decisions. Additionally, the company uses anonymous feedback tools to ensure that employees feel safe expressing concerns or suggesting new ideas. This formal feedback structure has allowed Zalando to stay agile and responsive to both employee and market needs, helping the company remain competitive in the fast-paced fashion industry.

Creating a Culture of Continuous Learning

Founders who are committed to overcoming blind spots must also embrace a mindset of continuous learning. By adopting a learning-oriented mindset, founders can identify blind spots early and adapt quickly to changing circumstances.

One of the biggest challenges for founders is recognising that they don't have all the answers. Humility is essential for overcoming blind spots, as it allows founders to acknowledge their limitations and seek out advice or expertise from others. Founders who cultivate humility are more likely to welcome feedback, embrace change, and continuously improve their decision-making process.

While founders need to have conviction in their vision, they must also remain open to alternative ideas and approaches. Finding the right balance between confidence and humility is key to avoiding blind spots. Founders who are overly rigid in their thinking risk missing out on valuable insights or new opportunities. On the other hand, founders who are too easily swayed may lose sight of their core mission.

Founders can maintain conviction in their vision while staying open to change by adopting a mindset of "strong opinions, loosely held." This approach allows founders to advocate passionately for their ideas but remain willing to adjust their course when presented with new evidence or feedback. Additionally, founders should regularly assess whether their original assumptions still hold true in light of changing market conditions or new data.

Chapter 24
The Future of Founder Mode: What's Next?

As we look toward the future, the concept of founder mode will continue to play a critical role in shaping how businesses are led and managed. In an increasingly complex and fast-changing world, founders who embrace the core principles of founder mode—customer obsession, bold decision-making, innovation, and resilience—will be better equipped to navigate the evolving landscape. However, the future of founder mode is not just about maintaining the status quo. It is about how founders will adapt and evolve these principles in the face of new challenges and opportunities, especially with the rapid advances in technology, changing societal expectations, and global disruptions.

In this concluding chapter, we will explore how founder mode is likely to evolve in the coming years, particularly in the context of emerging technologies such as artificial intelligence, automation, and decentralised platforms. We will discuss how founders can harness these advancements to continue driving innovation, maintain a customer-first approach, and foster sustainable business practices that align with societal and environmental goals.

Jon Smith

Embracing Technological Innovation as a Core Tenet

The pace of technological advancement shows no signs of slowing, and founders who stay ahead of these changes will have a significant advantage in shaping the future of their industries. Artificial intelligence (AI), blockchain, automation, and the Internet of Things (IoT) are just a few examples of technologies that are rapidly transforming how businesses operate and interact with customers. The future of founder mode will require an even greater emphasis on understanding and integrating these technologies into the core of business operations.

Founders of the future will need to be adept at leveraging AI and automation to enhance decision-making, streamline operations, and create personalised customer experiences. AI-powered analytics can provide founders with deeper insights into customer behaviour, market trends, and operational efficiencies. Automation will also play a key role in optimising processes, allowing founders to scale their businesses more efficiently while freeing up time for strategic thinking and innovation.

Daniel Dines, founder of UiPath, has been a pioneer in the field of robotic process automation (RPA), which uses AI and machine learning to automate repetitive tasks within businesses. UiPath's platform has been adopted by companies worldwide to improve productivity and reduce costs by automating routine workflows. Dines' focus on harnessing automation to drive efficiency has positioned UiPath as a leader in the automation space and demonstrates how founders can use emerging technologies to create scalable and innovative solutions.

Founder Mode in the Age of Decentralisation

Another significant trend shaping the future of founder mode is the rise of decentralisation. Blockchain technology and decentralised platforms are disrupting traditional industries by creating new business models that remove intermediaries and empower individuals and communities. Founders who adopt a decentralised approach can build businesses that are more transparent, equitable, and responsive to customer needs.

The future of founder mode will likely see the emergence of decentralised business models that shift power away from centralised authorities and toward users and communities. This can lead to greater trust, increased customer engagement, and more innovative approaches to value creation. Founders will need to rethink traditional hierarchical structures and explore new ways of organising their businesses that leverage the benefits of decentralisation.

Hayden Adams, founder of Uniswap, created one of the largest decentralised finance (DeFi) platforms that enables users to trade cryptocurrencies directly, without the need for a centralised exchange. Uniswap operates on the Ethereum blockchain, allowing users to provide liquidity and earn rewards in a decentralised, community-driven ecosystem. Adams' work with Uniswap demonstrates how founders can leverage blockchain technology to create new forms of value exchange that bypass traditional gatekeepers. The decentralised nature of Uniswap also gives users more control over their assets, aligning with the growing demand for transparency and autonomy in financial systems.

Sustainability and Social Responsibility: The New Imperatives for Founders

As societal expectations shift, founders are increasingly expected to lead with a focus on sustainability, social responsibility, and ethical business practices. Climate change, resource scarcity, and growing awareness of social inequality are placing pressure on companies to do more than simply generate profits. The future of founder mode will be defined by founders who can balance profitability with a strong commitment to environmental stewardship and positive social impact.

Founders will need to integrate sustainability into every aspect of their business, from product design to supply chain management to corporate governance. This requires a long-term perspective and a willingness to invest in initiatives that may not have immediate financial returns but are critical for the future of the planet and society. Founders who lead with purpose and create businesses that address global challenges will build stronger brands and earn the loyalty of customers, employees, and investors.

The Rise of Remote-First Companies and Global Talent Pools

The global lockdown accelerated the shift toward remote work, and many companies are now embracing remote-first or hybrid work models. The future of founder mode will see founders leading increasingly distributed teams, tapping into global talent pools, and creating flexible work environments that prioritise work-life balance and employee well-being. This shift will require founders to rethink traditional office structures, communication methods, and team management practices.

Founders who embrace remote work and global talent will have access to a broader range of skills and perspectives, enabling them to build more diverse and innovative teams. However, managing remote teams requires a different set of leadership skills, including fostering strong communication, maintaining team cohesion, and ensuring that employees feel connected to the company's mission and values.

Matt Mullenweg, founder of Automattic, the company behind WordPress, has been a pioneer in the remote work movement. Automattic operates as a fully distributed company, with employees working from locations around the world. Mullenweg has built a culture of trust and autonomy, where employees are empowered to work independently while staying connected through asynchronous communication and regular team meetups. Automattic's success demonstrates that remote-first companies can thrive and build strong, collaborative cultures even without a central office.

Founders as Agents of Change

In the past, the primary focus of many founders was to grow their companies, capture market share, and increase profitability. However, the next generation of founders is increasingly positioning themselves as agents of change—entrepreneurs who aim to make a positive impact on society while building financially successful businesses. These founders are not only solving problems for their customers but are also addressing broader social and environmental challenges, from inequality and diversity to climate change and access to healthcare.

Founders of the future will place a stronger emphasis on purpose-driven leadership, recognising that customers, employees, and investors are increasingly expecting companies to play a positive role in society. The ability to align business goals with broader societal missions will be a key differentiator for founders in the years to come. Purpose-driven founders will focus on long-term impact, ensuring that their companies are not just profitable but also responsible stewards of the environment and society.

Jessica O. Matthews, founder of Uncharted Power, is a prime example of a next-generation founder who is leading with purpose. Uncharted Power is a renewable energy company that focuses on harnessing kinetic energy to provide sustainable power solutions, particularly in underserved communities. Matthews has combined technological innovation with a mission to create equitable access to energy, addressing both environmental and social issues. Her leadership demonstrates how founders can leverage business to drive meaningful change in the world while building a successful enterprise.

Inclusive Leadership and Building Diverse Teams

As companies expand their reach globally, founders must prioritise diversity of thought, experience, and background to drive innovation and better understand the needs of a diverse customer base. Inclusive leadership goes beyond representation—it involves creating environments where all employees feel valued, heard, and empowered to contribute to the company's success.

Numerous studies have shown that diverse teams are more innovative, make better decisions, and drive stronger financial performance. Founders who prioritise diversity and inclusion from the outset will be better equipped to develop products and services that meet the needs of a broader range of customers. Moreover, inclusive leadership helps foster a culture of collaboration, creativity, and mutual respect, which is critical for attracting and retaining top talent.

Frederik Groce, co-founder of BLCK VC, is helping to reshape the venture capital landscape by advocating for greater diversity in startup investing. BLCK VC is an organisation dedicated to increasing the representation of Black investors in venture capital, with the goal of ensuring that underrepresented founders have access to the funding and resources they need to succeed. Groce's work highlights the importance of fostering diversity at all levels of the startup ecosystem, from investment to leadership. By championing inclusive leadership, founders like Groce are helping to create a more equitable and innovative business environment.

Adaptive Leadership in the Face of Uncertainty

The world is becoming increasingly complex and uncertain, with global events such as climate change, pandemics, geopolitical tensions, and technological disruption creating new challenges for businesses. The next generation of founders must be highly adaptive, capable of leading through uncertainty and making decisions with limited information. This requires a mindset of resilience, flexibility, and openness to change, as well as the ability to pivot quickly in response to new circumstances.

Founders will need to embrace agile leadership practices, where they can iterate quickly, test new ideas, and adjust their strategies as market conditions evolve. They must also cultivate resilience—not only within themselves but within their teams and organisations. Founders who can build resilient companies that are able to withstand shocks and bounce back from setbacks will be better positioned to succeed in an unpredictable world.

Henrique Dubugras and Pedro Franceschi, co-founders of Brex, demonstrated adaptive leadership when they pivoted their company during the COVID-19 pandemic. Brex, a fintech startup that provides corporate credit cards and financial services to startups, was initially focused on high-growth tech companies. However, when the pandemic hit, many of their target customers were negatively affected. Dubugras and Franceschi quickly adapted by expanding Brex's services to more traditional small and medium-sized businesses, helping them navigate the financial challenges of the pandemic. Their ability to pivot and adapt to changing market conditions allowed Brex to not only survive the crisis but emerge stronger.

Adaptive leadership is essential in a rapidly changing world. Founders who can pivot quickly, iterate on their strategies, and build resilience within their companies will be better equipped to navigate uncertainty and capitalise on new opportunities.

Leveraging Data and AI for Smarter Decision-Making

As technology continues to advance, the ability to harness data and artificial intelligence (AI) for smarter decision-making will become increasingly important for founders. The next generation of founders will need to be data-driven leaders who can use advanced analytics to gain insights into customer behaviour, optimise operations, and drive innovation. AI will also enable founders to make more informed and predictive decisions, allowing them to stay ahead of the competition.

Stephane Kasriel, founder of Upwork, has used data and AI to revolutionise the freelance marketplace. Upwork's platform leverages AI to match freelancers with clients based on their skills, experience, and project requirements, improving the efficiency and quality of the hiring process. Kasriel's focus on using data and technology to enhance the user experience has helped Upwork become a leader in the gig economy, providing new opportunities for remote workers and businesses alike. His leadership demonstrates how founders can harness the power of data and AI to drive innovation and scale.

Afterword

As we've explored throughout *Founder Mode: Leading with Resilience, Vision, and Purpose*, the founder's journey is a delicate balance of bold decision-making, hands-on leadership, and strategic evolution. Every founder faces the unique challenge of staying deeply connected to their vision while guiding their company toward sustainable growth. Resilience is what allows you to push through obstacles, but it's vision and purpose that ensure your efforts align with the long-term legacy you're striving to create.

This book has shown that the qualities of *Founder Mode*—passion, persistence, and purpose—are the driving forces behind successful founders who dare to disrupt industries and build companies that leave a lasting mark. But as your company grows, so must your leadership. The key is knowing when to lean in and when to evolve, empowering others without losing the entrepreneurial spirit that sparked your company's success.

Throughout your journey, remember that *Founder Mode* is not just about doing—it's about becoming. It's about transforming from a hands-on founder into a visionary leader capable of scaling both your company and your impact. It's about staying relentlessly committed to your values while adapting to the demands of growth.

As you step into the future, take the lessons from this book and apply them to your own leadership style. Embrace the resilience needed to weather the inevitable storms. Hold onto your vision as the guiding light for every decision. And, most importantly, lead with purpose, ensuring that your business not only grows but thrives in a way that reflects your passion and mission.

Now, it's time to activate your *Founder Mode*. It's time to scale, innovate, and create the lasting impact you've always envisioned. The world is ready for what you have to offer—are you ready to lead with resilience, vision, and purpose?

About the Author

Jon Smith is an entrepreneur and business strategist with a track record of founding, scaling, and leading companies to success. Part of the start-up team for Amazon Europe, Jon held leadership positions in major e-commerce and SaaS organisations, including Kitbag.com (acquired by Kleeneze), Book Depository (acquired by Amazon), and Autocab (acquired by Uber).

In addition to his work with large enterprises, Jon founded Toytopia, a thriving e-commerce venture he successfully exited after growing it into an international brand. Currently he provides fractional CMO services through GrowthWeaver and is the founder and CEO of Colugo Candles, an eco-luxury e-commerce start-up.

www.jonsmith.net

www.colugocandles.com

Founder Mode Reading List: Elevate Your Leadership Skills

Emotional Intelligence and Self-Awareness

Emotional Intelligence 2.0 by Travis Bradberry & Jean Greaves (2020, TalentSmart)

EQ Applied: The Real-World Guide to Emotional Intelligence by Justin Bariso (2021, Relativity Press)

Resilience and Overcoming Challenges

Resilient: How to Overcome Anything and Build a Stronger Future by Seamus Gillen (2021, Lid Publishing)

Unstoppable: How to Overcome Adversity to Achieve Greatness by Ben Angel (2020, Entrepreneur Press)

Visionary Leadership

The Vision-Driven Leader by Michael Hyatt (2020, Baker Books)

Radical Vision by Bernie Swain (2021, Matt Holt Books)

Adaptability and Agility

The Adaptation Advantage by Heather McGowan & Chris Shipley (2020, Wiley)

Leading Through Disruption by Andrew Harrison (2021, Bloomsbury Business)

Customer Obsession

Customer-Driven Transformation by Joe Heapy (2020, Kogan Page)

Winning on Purpose by Fred Reichheld (2021, Harvard Business Review Press)

Innovation and Product Development

Loonshots by Safi Bahcall (2020, St. Martin's Press)

The Innovation Stack by Jim McKelvey (2020, Portfolio)

Delegation and Scaling Leadership

Who Not How by Dan Sullivan & Dr. Benjamin Hardy (2020, Hay House Business)

Scaling Leadership by Robert J. Anderson & William A. Adams (2021, Wiley)

Purpose-Driven Leadership

Leading with Purpose by Marc Koehler (2021, CreateSpace Independent Publishing)

The Purpose Factor by Brian Bosché & Gabrielle Bosché (2020, Post Hill Press)

Risk-Taking & Bold Decision-Making

Risk Forward by Victoria Labalme (2021, Page Two)

Lea by Howard Yu (2020, PublicAffairs)

Entrepreneurship

Traction: Get a Grip on Your Business by Gino Wickman (2021, BenBella Books)

The Lean Startup: How Today's Entrepreneurs Use Continuous Innovation by Eric Ries (2020, Crown Business)

High Growth Handbook: Scaling Startups from 10 to 10,000 People by Elad Gil (2020, Stripe Press)

Zero to One: Notes on Startups, or How to Build the Future by Peter Thiel (2020, Currency)

Marketing & Growth

Hook Point: How to Stand Out in a 3-Second World by Brendan Kane (2020, Hay House)

Hacking Growth: How Today's Fastest-Growing Companies Drive Breakout Success by Sean Ellis & Morgan Brown (2020, Crown Business)

Building a StoryBrand: Clarify Your Message So Customers Will Listen by Donald Miller (2020, HarperCollins Leadership)

Contagious: How to Build Word of Mouth in the Digital Age by Jonah Berger (2020, Simon & Schuster)

Note from the author

Hi,

Thanks so much for reading *Founder Mode: Leading with Resilience, Vision, and Purpose.*

If you think others would benefit from reading this book, whilst on their own founder or management journey, I would be incredibly grateful if you'd be so kind as to leave a review.

Reviews really help authors for a number of reasons, not least, providing feedback on what readers like, and improving visibility of the book on online retail sites.

Thanks in advance and once again I wish you well in your business endeavours.

Jon Smith

www.ingramcontent.com/pod-product-compliance
Lightning Source LLC
Chambersburg PA
CBHW041209220326
41597CB00030BA/5167